THE MEDIATION OF CHRIST

The Mediation of Christ

THOMAS F TORRANCE

HELMERS & HOWARD
COLORADO SPRINGS

This edition published under license from
T&T Clark, 59 George Street, Edinburgh EH2 2LQ, Scotland

by Helmers & Howard, Publishers, Inc
PO Box 7407, Colorado Springs, CO 80933, USA

First published in Great Britain by
Paternoster Press, 1983 and in the USA by
W. B. Eerdmans Publishing Company 1984
This revised edition published 1992

ISBN 0-939443-50-3

Library of Congress Cataloging-in-Publication Data
Torrance, Thomas Forsyth, 1913-
The Mediation of Christ / Thomas F. Torrance. – 2nd ed.
p. cm.
Originally published: Grand Rapids : W.B. Eerdmans Pub. Co., 1984
ISBN 0-939443-50-3 :
1. Jesus Christ—Mediation. I. Title.
BT255. T67 1992   91-41856
232 .8—dc20   CIP

Printed in the United States of America.

Contents

To
Alison, our beloved daughter

Preface

The purpose of these lectures is to help students, ministers and pastors, and other Church leaders and workers, to think theologically about the Gospel, so that they may get a firmer grip upon its content for their various ministries. The material presented here relates to earlier addresses on the Mediation of Christ given at Summer Schools of Theology in St Andrews, Scotland and Princeton, New Jersey, which were naturally adapted to the circumstances, conditions and needs of the people who attended them. This book represents an extended form of the Didsbury Lectures which it was my privilege to deliver in The British Isles Nazarene College in Manchester during October 1982. I would like to express my warm gratitude for the kindness accorded to me by the staff and students of the College, and not least for the friendship of the Dean of the College, the Rev. T. A. Noble, whom I got to know first during his own theological studies at Edinburgh University when he distinguished himself in Biblical, Patristic and Dogmatic theology in a way that won the deep admiration of his teachers. For once I have dispensed with references and historical notes, in the hope that a more straightforward presentation of my exposition will be of help to a wider ministry of the Gospel in preaching and teaching alike.

My wife and I have been marvellously blessed with a very dear daughter, Alison, whose love and thoughtful care for us are beyond measure. This book is dedicated to her in token of our unbounded thankfulness and joy.

Canty Bay,
East Lothian
October, 1982   THOMAS F. TORRANCE

Foreword to New Edition

In this new edition of *The Mediation of Christ* I have inserted some sub-titles into the third and fourth chapters, to facilitate their reading, and added a new chapter on 'The Atonement and the Holy Trinity'. This is intended to say something about the place and necessity of a doctrine of the atonement for a doctrine of the Trinity, but also to show that the doctrine of the Trinity is necessary for a proper doctrine of Atonement. In relating this presentation to the discussion in earlier chapters, I have continued to pay attention to the problem of dualism in theology, by showing its damaging effect in an ultra transcendentalist conception of God, and in splitting apart the doctrine of the one God from the doctrine of the triune God. I have also developed further the way in which the mission of Israel and the mission of Christ are deeply interlocked in faithful understanding of revelation and reconciliation, particularly in the way in which Jews and Christians need one another in seeking to understand more of the way in which God has given us access to know him through himself and in himself. I hope this will make the book more complete in drawing out further the movement of atoning propitation between God and man, in the way in which we are given access to the Father through the cross of Christ and the communion of the Holy Spirit. I have also offered discussion of this subject in the book *The Witness of the Jews to God*, edited by my brother, the Rev. David W. Torrance, published in 1982 by the Handsel Press, Edinburgh.

I have been greatly encouraged by the reception given to my book on both sides of the Atlantic, not least by lay people who have found healing and freedom in this way of understanding the mediatorial work of the Lord Jesus Christ and the way his faithfulness in vicarious activity undergirds the response of faith called forth from us through his mediation of the Holy Spirit. Some people evidently feel that the stress I have laid upon unconditional grace undermines the integrity of the response we are called to make in repentance for sin and in acceptance of Jesus Christ as our personal Saviour. Part of the problem here is that unconditional grace is too costly, for it calls in question all that we are and do, so that even in our repenting and believing we cannot rely upon our own response but only upon the response Christ has offered to the Father in our place and on our behalf. How the 'I' of the human believer and the 'I' of Christ are related to one another, expressed for example in the Pauline statement, 'I, yet not I but Christ', is a miracle of the Spirit, and is ultimately as inexplicable as the miracle of the Virgin Birth of Jesus which for me is the unique God-given pattern of unconditional grace. All through the incarnate life and activity of the Lord Jesus we are shown that 'all of grace' does not mean 'nothing of man', but precisely the opposite: *all of grace means all of man*, for the fullness of grace creatively includes the fullness and completeness of our human response in the equation. But this is not something that can be understood logically, for logically 'all of grace' would mean 'nothing of man', which may tempt people to apportion the role of Christ and of the believer by arguing for 'something of grace' and 'something of man', something done *for me* by Christ and something I do *for myself*! *All* of grace means *all* of man! We must remember that in all his healing and saving relations with us Jesus Christ is engaged in personalising and humanising (never depersonalising or dehumanising) activity, so that in all our relations with him we are made more truly and fully human in our personal response of faith than ever before. This takes place in us through the creative activity of the Holy Spirit as he unites us to the perfect humanity of the Lord Jesus conceived by the Holy Spirit, born of the Virgin Mary and raised again from the dead. The miracle of faith and new birth takes place in us after the pattern of the Virgin Birth of Jesus himself and his resurrection from the grave. It is not that our response to Christ takes effect in us only as it is under our own disposal, or under the determination of our own will (the very self-will which Christ calls us to renounce!), any more than the effect of the unconditional grace of the Lord Jesus Christ or the power of his risen life can come under our own disposing. All of grace really does mean all of man. How could the unconditional grace of the Lord Jesus Christ, crucified and risen again for us, how could 'all of Christ', ever mean a depreciating of the very humanity he came to save?!

In some ways we have here much the same problem that has arisen in the minds of several reviewers who think, when they read my attempt to expound without hedging the teaching of the New Testament that Christ died for all people, that this is to put forward a doctrine of 'universal salvation', as opposed to a doctrine of 'limited atonement'. This implies, however, that there is a logical relation between the death of Jesus on the cross and the forgiveness of our sins: if Jesus died for all people, then logically all people must be saved; but if some people go to hell, then logically Christ did not die for them. This rationalist way of thinking about the atonement is very sad, for what it actually does is to substitute a logical relation for the activity of the Holy Spirit in accounting for the efficacy of the blood of Christ. The atoning death of Christ is to be approached with the greatest reverence and awe as holy mystery ultimately grounded in the infinite being of God. The reason for the atonement, its why and its how, is hidden in the holy love of God, before which the very angels veil their faces and which they shield from our prying minds.

Again it is the same mistake people made when they try to offer a logical reason why some persons believe and why some persons strangely do not believe in Christ or reject him, like Judas, for example, who after receiving the supreme pledge of Christ's redeeming love at the last Supper, went out and betrayed him. How could he do that? How is that to be explained? Evil whenever and however it arises entails a radical break or discontinuity in our relations with God, which in the nature of the case just cannot be explained, for any attempted explanation would draw a line of logical continuity across the break and rationalise its discontinuity away. If that were the case, if there were no abysmal, that is bottomless, chasm of evil, then the cross of Christ is a hollow sham, and in that event God incarnate need not have given himself in atoning sacrifice for sin. God does not offer us any explanation for evil, but deals decisively and finally with it by entering himself into its abysmal chasm separating us from him and bridging it through the atoning life and death of his incarnate Son. At the same time the fact that God himself had to make atonement in order to save us, reveals the bottomless nature of the discontinuity between man and God which nothing else and no one else could bridge.

It is my hope and prayer that this final chapter on 'The Atonement and the Holy Trinity' will help readers toward godly and reverent thinking in their approach to the ineffable mystery of the cross of Christ.

I am deeply grateful to Dr Geoffrey Green of T. and T. Clark Ltd., the Edinburgh Publishers, for readily agreeing to produce this new edition. The theological world continues to be immensely indebted to him and his devoted staff for all they do in the production of Christian literature.

Thomas F. Torrance,
37 Braid Farm Road,
Edinburgh EH10 6LE
February 1991

CHAPTER ONE

The Mediation of Revelation

From time to time there have arisen in the course of human culture ways of thinking in which aspects of reality that are naturally integrated have been torn apart from each other, with damaging effect in different areas of knowledge. Thus in the great European tradition of analytical thought, which derives from classical Greece, a habit of mind became widely entrenched in which the sensible appearances of things were abstracted from the intelligible base in which they were grounded, with disastrous consequences, as we have discovered, in philosophy and science, for it meant that knowledge of reality was artificially cut short at appearances and what we can logically deduce from our critical observations of them. That is a state of affairs which in this century our science has been struggling to overcome, and the measure of its startling advance in recent decades is the measure of its success in recovering a more natural, integrated approach to the investigation of the universe.

One of the benefits of this closer readjustment of scientific method to nature has been to show us something of the damage which dichotomous ways of thinking have done to our knowledge of God, and not least to our knowledge of God in Jesus Christ. Their effect has been to detach Jesus Christ from God, to detach Jesus Christ from Israel, and to detach Christianity from Christ himself. Now when that sort of thing happens, the very essence of the Christian Gospel is at stake. In people's understanding a deep split is introduced

into the mediation between God and man, and the Person of
the Mediator is torn apart from God's self-revelation to
mankind and uprooted from his redemptive purpose in
history. That was in fact the crucial problem that faced the
Christian Church in the early centuries of its existence, when
dualist presuppositions in the cultural framework of the
ancient world threatened to disrupt its proclamation of Jesus
Christ as the Son of God come in the flesh (1 John 4:1-15), and
the Church found itself engaged in a hard theological struggle to preserve the New Testament teaching that 'there is one
God, and one Mediator between God and man, the man
Christ Jesus, who gave himself a ransom for all' (1 Tim. 2:15).
It is basically the same problem that we have to deal with
today, for the Church is once again engaged in a theological
struggle to conserve evangelical faith in the oneness between
what God is toward us in Jesus Christ and what he is in his
own Being as God. If that relation in being and agency is cut,
then the whole Gospel of saving mediation between God and
man collapses.

Epistemologically, the problem to be faced in ancient or
modern times can be posed in this way. In the analytic
tradition of thought there takes place an abstraction of Jesus
Christ from the matrix of natural or inherent relations in
which he is found, and then an abstraction of the external
appearance of Christ from the objective frame of event and
significance with which he is bound up in the Gospel.
Epistemologically — other things being equal — this is the
same question which, as I have already indicated, we have
tried to resolve in other fields of human inquiry when we
have had to turn away from the severely analytical and
abstractive modes of thought inherited from classical physics and observational science, and develop dynamic, relational and holistic ways of thinking more in accordance with
the modes of connection and behaviour actually found in
nature, to which we have been directed by the epoch-making
work of James Clerk Maxwell and Albert Einstein above all.
Now when we adopt this kind of approach in scientific
inquiry, we investigate things in their interrelations with one
another where relations between things have to do with

what they actually are. But at the same time we seek to understand things in the light of their internal relations in virtue of which they are what they really are in their inherent constitutive structures whereby they are distinguished from other things. Neither of these forms of investigation can be pursued properly apart from the other. As I see it, it is along these lines that our modern knowledge of the universe has been built up through particle physics and astrophysics, with such astonishing results.

Undoubtedly this advance into a deeper and more natural way of understanding things, which applies to all areas of knowledge, cannot but have a bearing upon theological inquiry. So far as our knowledge of Jesus Christ is concerned, this suggests that we should adopt a two-fold approach. On the one hand, we should seek to understand Christ within the actual matrix of interrelations from which he sprang as Son of David and Son of Mary, that is, in terms of his intimate bond with Israel in its covenant relationship with God throughout history. On the other hand, however, we should seek to understand Christ, not by way of observational deductions from his appearances, but in the light of what he is in himself in his internal relations with God, that is, in terms of his intrinsic significance disclosed through his self-witness and self-communication to us in word and deed and reflected through the evangelical tradition of the Gospel in the medium which he created for this purpose in the apostolic foundation of the Church.

When we adopt this kind of approach, whether in natural science or in theology, we find that progress in understanding is necessarily circular. We develop a form of inquiry in which we allow some field of reality to disclose itself to us in the complex of its internal relations or its latent structure, and thus seek to understand it in the light of its own intrinsic intelligibility or *logos*. As we do that we come up with a significant clue in the light of which all evidence is then re-examined and reinterpreted and found to fall into a coherent pattern of order. Thus we seek to understand something, not by schematising it to an external or alien framework of thought, but by operating with a framework of thought appropriate to it, one which it suggests to us out of its own inherent constitutive relations and which we are rationally constrained to adopt in faithful understanding and interpretation of it.

I sometimes liken the procedure that this involves to the sort of thing we do when we have solved a jig-saw puzzle. In the first instance we have to find out how to fit the scattered pieces together, when the picture which they conjointly make comes to view. But after that, when the picture is broken up and the various pieces have been thrown back into disarray, it is quite impossible for us to fit them all together again as though we did not know the picture that they made. Something like that happens in the process of scientific inquiry. Once we have got hold of the basic clue or gained some anticipatory insight into the pattern of things, we set about re-examining and reinterpreting all the data, putting them together under the guidance of the basic insight we have discovered until the full coherent pattern comes clearly to view. Now of course in a scientific inquiry the fundamental insight with which we work may have to be revised as all the pieces of evidence come together and throw light upon each other, but nevertheless it is under the direction of that insight that the discovery is made. Once the insight has put us on the track of that discovery, something irreversible has taken place in our understanding: a pattern of truth has been built into our minds on which we cannot go back, and which we cannot rationally deny.

Now I submit that a process of deepening understanding rather like that took place in the New Testament community and in the early Church, not of course in any formal scientific way but in a profoundly natural and intuitive way. When the crucified Jesus rose again from the dead and poured out his Spirit at Pentecost, the intrinsic significance of his Person and all he had said and done broke forth in its self-evidencing power and seized hold of the Church as the very Word or *Logos* of God. Looking back we can say that the Apostles and Fathers came upon a basic insight in the light of which the whole saving Event of Jesus Christ came to be understood out of its intrinsic intelligibility and within the framework of objective meaning which it created for itself in the context of Israel. The fundamental clue with which they operated was the oneness of Jesus Christ, the Jew from Bethlehem and Nazareth, with God the Father on the one hand and with the unique fact and history of Israel among the nations on the other hand. Within that complex of interrelations they found themselves coming to grips with the essential message of the Gospel embodied in Jesus in its relation to the age-old message of God that had been worked out in his covenant partnership with Israel, and discovered that it was a message for the salvation of all mankind. In that mediation of God's saving revelation the startling events in the life, death and resurrection of Jesus fell into place within a divinely ordered pattern of grace and truth, and the bewildering enigma of Jesus himself became disclosed: he was incarnate Son of God and Saviour of the world.

Our immediate concern in this chapter is to consider the mediation of Christ from the perspective of his intimate and intense involvement with Israel, in the hope that we may gain a fresh understanding of the mediation between God and man as it became grounded in humanity through God's anguished struggle with Israel and as it was brought to its decisive fulfilment in the Incarnation. In probing into the developing structure of mediation as it took shape within the frame of Israel's distinctive worship of God and its priestly mission to mankind, we find a divine intention persistently at work which has to do both with revelation and with reconciliation. While these are really inseparable, for the purposes of our discussion we shall be concerned in this chapter more with the mediation of revelation, and in the following chapter more with the mediation of reconciliation.

What are the tools we need in order to grasp the content of divine revelation? Appropriate tools are needed for the knowledge of God, just as we need tools for almost everything else, for making things and shaping them, and even tools for making tools, which I find rather instructive. Think of the machine-tool industry which is one of the most important industries in the modern world. A few years ago I had a meeting with a group of research scientists in

industry, some of whom were engaged in the work of
devising and making very sensitive, complex instruments. I
was quite astonished when one of them explained the kind
of tools he was making for a university department of high
energy physics, for it was quite clear that in order to make
those tools he had not only to know as much about high
energy physics as the physicists who ordered the tools, but
had himself to engage in a good deal of original research and
make fresh discoveries in order to provide those physicists
with the kind of tools that would really advance their
research. I thought a lot about that, for it brought home to me
the fact that, while science and technology are not to be
confounded, all science and not least pure science, is engaged in the construction of appropriate tools with which to
shape knowledge and understanding of what is being
investigated. What I have in mind here are not physical or
electronic tools but conceptual tools. Really to get to know
something we need to find the appropriate way in which to
grasp it and shape what we grasp in our mind—that is to say,
what we need are adequate modes of thought and speech.
The need for conceptual tools of this kind is particularly
pressing when we have to do with something radically new
which we cannot understand by assimilating it into the
framework of what we already know, and for which old
patterns of thought and speech are not only inadequate but
can prove quite false. Quite new disclosures of nature
require new modes of thought and speech to match them.
That is why again and again as scientific inquiry opens up
new ground and quite unanticipated discoveries are made,
it has to forge new mental instruments and invent new
symbolic languages, and why if they are really matched to
the hitherto unknown aspects of nature they open out the
possibility of still further discovery.

I believe that this applies no less to our knowledge of God.
If we are to know him and speak about him in a way that is
appropriate to him, we need to have fitting modes of thought
and speech, adequate conceptual forms and structures, and
indeed reverent and worthy habits of worship and behaviour governing our approach to him. Let us consider God's

historical relations with the people of Israel in just this light. And let us think of it, for a moment rather anthropo-morphically, in this way. In his desire to reveal himself and make himself knowable to mankind, he selected one small race out of the whole mass of humanity, and subjected it to intensive interaction and dialogue with himself in such a way that he might mould and shape this people in the service of his self-revelation. Recall Jeremiah's analogy of the potter at work with his clay, which is so apt here. He takes a lump of clay, throws it down upon the potter's wheel, and pro-ceeds to rotate it under the steady pressure of his fingers until it is moulded into the kind of vessel suitable for his purpose. But when the clay proves to be lumpy and recalcitrant he breaks it down and remoulds it in accordance with his design, and he does that again and again until he has formed and fashioned a vessel to his liking which will serve his purpose well. That is how the prophets, and St Paul also, regarded Israel, as clay in the hands of the divine Potter which he subjects to his will, yet not in the mechanical way of a human potter with his impersonal handiwork but in the way in which a father imparts distinctive characteristics to his offspring. Thus God established a special partnership of covenanted kinship with Israel, so that within the intimate structure of family relations he might increasingly imprint himself upon the generations of Israel in such a way that it could become the instrument of his great purpose of revelation.

Far from being restricted to the people of Israel itself, that was a purpose which God had for all mankind, for he took Israel into his hands in this unique way in order to provide the actual means, a whole set of spiritual tools, appropriate forms of understanding, worship and expression, through which apprehension of God could be made accessible to human beings and knowledge of God could take root in the soil of humanity. A two-way movement was involved: an adaptation of divine revelation to the human mind and an adaptation of articulate forms of human understanding and language to divine revelation. That is surely how we are to regard God's long historical dialogue with Israel: the penetration of the Word of God into the depths of Israel's being and soul in such a way that it took human shape and yet in such a way that the human response it called forth was so locked into the Word in God that it was used as the vehicle of further address on the part of that Word to Israel. That ever-deepening, spiral movement of God's self-revelation to Israel was far from being an easy or painless process. The Old Testament Scriptures, which are the product of it, show that Israel was subjected to the most appalling suffering, an ordeal in which Israel was again and again broken upon the wheel of divine Providence in order to become pliable and serviceable within the movement of God's intimate self-giving and self-communicating to it as a people set apart for that end.

Throughout that harrowing experience the covenant bond between God and Israel was steadily tightened and knotted into the existence of Israel as a people, which had the effect of making Israel stand out as an oddity among the other peoples of the earth, and of plunging it into internal upheaval whenever it chafed at its covenanted destiny. In the following chapter we shall consider what it meant for Israel to be used by God in the mediation of divine reconciliation, but at this point we must reflect on what it meant for Israel to have a unique role in the mediation of divine revelation. The fact that Israel was called to be the people 'entrusted with the oracles of God', which it could not be without embodying those oracles in its way of life, brought upon Israel intense suffering, physical and mental, in its relations with other peoples. But Israel had to suffer above all from God, precisely as the chosen medium of his self-revelation to mankind, for divine revelation was a fire in the mind and soul and memory of Israel burning away all that was in conflict with God's holiness, mercy and truth. By its very nature that revelation could not be faithfully appropriated and articulated apart from conflict with deeply ingrained habits of human thought and understanding and without the development of new patterns of thought and understanding and speech as worthy vehicles of its communication.

Throughout the long ordeal of Israel's historical and

religious encounter with the living God, in the course of which there took place a unique cultural integration of its thought and religion, its literature and its way of life, the Word of God was at work preparing the matrix for the final mediation of divine revelation to mankind, when the personal self-communication of God could be met by true and faithful reception from man. And at last in the fullness of time the Word of God became man in Jesus, born of the Virgin Mary, within the embrace of Israel's faith and worship and expectation, himself God and man, in whom the covenanted relationship between God and Israel and through Israel with all humanity was gathered up, transformed and fulfilled once for all. In him the revealing of God and the understanding of man fully coincided, the whole Word of God and the perfect response of man were indivisibly united in one Person, the Mediator, who was received, believed and worshipped together with God the Father and the Holy Spirit by the apostolic community which he creatively called forth and assimilated to his own mission from the Father. Thus as both the incarnate revelation of God and the embodied knowledge of God, Jesus Christ constitutes in himself the Way, the Truth and the Life through whom alone access to God the Father is freely open for all the peoples of mankind. That is to say, as the incarnate Word and Truth of God Jesus Christ in his own personal Being is identical with the Revelation which he mediates. But he is at the same time the very Way in which it is to be apprehended and interpreted and the very Life which is the light of men, for it is only through the assimilation of our minds to the Mind of God incarnate in Christ that we are given the modes of discernment, forms of thought, and the structures of the understanding which we need in order to grasp and articulate knowledge of God in a way that is worthy of him.

We must now consider rather more fully several aspects of this mediation of revelation in Christ in relation to the unique function and destiny of Israel in the whole movement of God's revealing purpose in history.

(1) *The covenant partnership between God and Israel involved a running conflict between divine revelation and what St Paul called 'the carnal mind'.*

Israel was not chosen by God because of any special religious propensity or insight which it might have, for it was not different in this respect from any other people. Nor was it chosen because it was morally or spiritually worse than any other people, for that was not the case either. However, within the covenant relationship in which God drew near to Israel and Israel was drawn near to God in an unprecedentedly intimate way, the innate resistance of the human soul and mind resulting from the alienation of man from God inevitably became intensified, so that again and again the rebellion of Israel against God appears to have been in inverse proportion to the favour of God lavished upon it. Within the moral and liturgical institutions of the covenant, the revelation of the nature of God as holy and righteous, as truth and love, was brought to bear upon the whole way of Israel's life and thought, when it was found to cut against the grain of its natural existence, even against the grain of its religious desires and forms of worship, as we can see above all in the incessant conflict between the worship of Jahweh and the cult of the Baalim and Ashtaroth, that is, between the worship of God the Father and the worship of nature and sex, which is reflected all through the pages of the Old Testament. Yet that is what objective divine revelation had to do in opening up the way through all in-built bias against it for its realisation and actualisation within Israel, and in turning the soul and mind of this people inside out so that it was no longer self-centred but God-centred. However, even when divine revelation succeeded in its struggle against idolatry and mythology for the devotion and fidelity of Israel to the living God, and in so far as it won the soul and mind of this people, generating within it the most profound and sublime understanding of God that had yet arisen, there remained a kind of 'love-hate' relation between Israel and God. The more deeply the Word of God penetrated into the innermost depths of Israel's existence and embodied itself within it, the more it seemed to burn like fire in its bones until the great prophets who were burdened with the Word of the Lord cried out in agony. To be the bearer of divine revelation is to suffer, and not only to suffer but to be killed and made alive again, and not only to be made alive but to be continually renewed and refashioned under its creative impact. That is the pre-history of the crucifixion and resurrection of Jesus in Israel.

In the Hebrew idiom revelation implies not only the uncovering of God but the uncovering of the ear and heart of man to receive revelation. Thus the mediation of divine revelation through Israel has the effect not only of disclosing something of the nature of God but of disclosing the natural offence to God deeply embedded in the human heart. Now if this is the case, as we find in God's dealings with Israel, that the more deeply revelation pierces into the roots of human being the more it intensifies the enmity of the human heart against God, then the destined function of Israel in bearing and mediating divine revelation for mankind cannot but have the effect upon us of rousing and bringing to the surface our own latent enmity against God, which can easily express itself in the form of enmity to Israel. As we have noted, that is an enmity which Israel has always had to suffer from others, because it was taken into a special relation with God which affected the basic structure of its ways of life and thought and made it strange to them. Behind that lies the fact that the conflict between God and man throughout Israel's existence which contributed to its strangeness, mirrors the conflict between God and ourselves, which we resent, and while our real quarrel is with the searching light of divine revelation reflected by Israel, it is against Israel itself that we vent our resentment. There we have, I believe, the root of anti-semitism. But wherever and whenever anti-semitism arises it is a clear sign that people are engaged in conflict with God and with the same kind of conflict that left its mark upon Israel. No other people has ever engaged with God in the same depth or intensity of the contradiction between man and God as Israel. That is what makes it so difficult for other peoples to appreciate the role of Israel in the world, but if we find ourselves objecting to the Jews, what is really at issue is our conflict with God.

Israel teaches us, then, that divine revelation cuts against the grain of our naturalistic existence and calls into question the naturalistic patterns of human thought. If we are to know God in accordance with the way he has chosen through Israel to Christ — and now that he has actually taken it, there is no other way — we must let the sword of divine truth that was thrust into Israel pierce our own heart also so that its secret contradiction of God may be laid bare. We must go to school with Israel and share with it the painful transformation of its mind and soul which prepared it for the final mediation of God's self-revelation in Jesus Christ, if we ourselves are to break free from our assimilation to the patterns of this world and be transformed through the renewing of our mind in Christ, for only then will we be in a position to recognise, discern and appreciate what God wills to make known to us.

(2) The election of Israel by God took the form of a community of reciprocity.

As we have seen God mediates his revelation to human beings in such a way that he accommodates his self-revealing to human knowing and adapts human knowing to receive and apprehend what he reveals in ways that are appropriate to it. Thus the mediation of divine revelation took a spiral course throughout Israel's sacred history, for the Word of God came to Israel in such a creative way that it moulded the responses it called forth, assimilating them to its self-communication so that they served the deepening process of mutual adaptation between divine revelation and human understanding until the Word of God was built into the inner structure and continuity of Israel's existence and mission as a holy, priestly people in the midst of humankind.

Let us think of it in this way. All the relations which God establishes with us his children are of a reciprocal kind, as he makes very clear in presenting himself to us as One who hears and answers prayer and who gives us the freedom to come personally before him with our petitions. 'Ask and you will receive,' said Jesus, 'seek and you will find, knock and the door will be opened to you.' In fact ninety per cent of all that Jesus taught about prayer had to do with simple petition. Prayer involves a two-way movement between God and man. That is what Jesus exhibited in his own filial relation with the Father, into which he incorporates us, thereby making his own relation as Son to the heavenly Father the ground and pattern of our reciprocal relations with God. That is the kind of relationship which God had anticipated in the provisions of his covenant with Israel: 'I will be your Father, and you will be my son', and it was on that basis that the whole structure of Israel's approach to God in liturgy, psalm and service was constituted. The kind of reciprocity which the covenant envisaged, however, was of a corporate as well as of a personal nature, for personal relations with God took place within the corporate interaction of Israel with God. It is significant that when the Old Testament characterises the way in which God kept faith with his covenant people as 'steadfast love and truth', it should use the same expression to characterise the relations of the people of the covenant with one another, for the very bonds that bound the people of Israel to one another were the bonds with which God bound himself to Israel. The covenant partnership of God with Israel incorporated a brotherly covenant among the members of Israel, and that brotherly covenant was grounded in the covenant relations of God with Israel as a whole. Thus, so to speak, the vertical and the horizontal interrelations of the covenant partnership penetrated each other, constituting a coherent community of reciprocity between God and Israel, and manifesting a community response to the self-revealing and self-giving of God to Israel.

In seeking to understand the role of Israel in the mediation of revelation, therefore, we must consider, not just Jews, not just this or that prophet or this or that author in the Old Testament Scriptures, but Israel as a whole, 'all Israel', to use St Paul's expression, that is, Israel as a coherent entity before God. God mediated his revelation through the totality of Israel's existence and mission, for Israel came into being and has continued to remain what it is precisely as the corporate counterpart to the self-revelation and self-communication of God to mankind. This means that we must think of Israel itself as *the Prophet* sent by God, not just Isaiah, or Jeremiah, or Ezekiel, but Israel, while Isaiah, Jeremiah, Ezekiel and all the prophets are to be understood within the one body which had been brought into a special relationship with God within which it was moulded and structured as the earthen vessel to receive and communicate the Word of God to mankind. It was within Israel constituted in that way that God sent the prophets and out of Israel constituted in that way that the Holy Scriptures of the Old Testament were composed and handed down.

In mediating his revelation to mankind in this way through Israel God teaches us that revelation and the people called out of the world to receive and embody it, revelation and church, go inseparably together. I believe that it is in this light that we are still to understand Israel, even in modern times, in its profound spiritual and national struggle with its divine destiny. Unlike any other nation Israel is not just a nation, an *ethnos*, but a people of God, a *laos*. In virtue of Israel's 'peculiar' status and character, as a people chosen by the Lord out of all peoples on earth to be his special possession, a 'holy nation', Israel as a people is a kind of church, a community burdened with the knowledge of God, a community divinely adapted and constituted as the correlate of God's self-revelation. That is a very difficult role for Israel to fulfil in the modern world where once again it has to defend itself as an independent national entity, for as *laos* as well as ethnos Israel cannot behave as though it were only *ethnos*, a nation like the other nations of the earth, without conflicting with the basic relationship which underlies its whole history and existence. That is to say, Israel cannot completely nationalise its own existence without detaching itself from the very covenant with God which constitutes it the people that it always has been and is. Conversely, it is in the light of this modern predicament of Israel that we can understand somewhat better the difficult role which Israel had to fulfil in Old and New Testament times, as the priestly people entrusted with the deposit of divine revelation.

We may even be led to realise in a more discerning way

that the Old Testament Scriptures which have been handed down to us are not to be treated as free-floating divine oracles with an independent existence of their own, in spite of their written form, for they cannot properly be detached from their embodiment in the whole historical fact of Israel and its vicarious role in the reception and communication of the Word of God to the human race, not least in the incarnate form of Jesus Christ. But we may also learn from the way that God took with Israel that the New Testament Scriptures are to be understood, not as spaceless and timeless transcriptions of revelation, but as bound up with the apostolic foundation of the Church in which the mediation of God's self-revelation through Jesus Christ and in his Spirit became embodied, and therefore from within the structured coefficient or interpretative framework which that revelation created for itself within the Church to reflect its meaning and guide interpretation of its evangelical message. Certainly the New Testament does not offer an interpretation of itself except as the destined fulfilment of divine revelation mediated through Israel and except from within the incorporation of the Church as its revelatory counterpart within the commonwealth of Israel.

(3) *God's revelation came to Israel in such a way that it intersected and integrated its spiritual and physical reality.*

One of the most startling features about the Old Testament Scriptures is the way in which they represent the Word of God as becoming physically implicated with Israel in the very stuff of its earthy being and behaviour. Divine revelation did not just bear upon the life and culture of Israel in some tangential fashion, rippling the surface of its moral and religious consciousness, but penetrated into the innermost centre of Israel and involved itself in the concrete actuality and locality of its existence in time and space, so that in its articulated form as human word it struck home to Israel with incisive definiteness and specificity. That is something which we find difficult to understand when we operate with a dualist frame of thought at the back of our minds, for it makes us want to detach the religious concept of Israel from the particularity of its physical existence and history in space and time, and to peel away from divine revelation what we tend to regard as its transient physical clothing. That would be a fatal mistake. But now a change has been taking place in the framework of our modern thought which helps us to think rather differently: I refer to our realisation that there is no space without time and no time without space, for there is only space-time. God's revelation was mediated to Israel in the continuous indivisible field of space-time, in such a way that the physical configurations were inextricably interwoven with its communication and articulation to Israel. That is why, as we shall see, revelation and reconciliation had to go together.

What does this mean? Quite frankly, it means that if we are to understand and interpret divine revelation in the specific spatio-temporal forms which it assumed in and through Israel, we cannot detach the Old Testament Scriptures from the land any more than from the people of Israel. The people of the book and the people of the land belong inseparably together, for they have been forged together by the way that God himself has taken in the actualisation and the dynamic course of his covenant partnership with Israel. What happens when the inner constitutive connections between people, land and revelation are severed, can be seen from what happened to Judaism when the Jews themselves suffered radical detachment from the spatio-temporal milieu of God's self-revelation. Judaism tended to become an abstract ethical religion, largely bereft of its all-important priestly and redemptive tradition and characterised by a serious loss of relevance in space and time. Something very different is to be found in Judaism today, the Judaism of Israel in Israel, where a reverse process is taking place, as the ancient people of God struggles to recover its lost concreteness, something much more than a kosher way of life, symbolic as that is of the fact that physical behaviour is tied up with faith in God. This has to do with a radical change in the soul and mind of Israel as the Torah and the Promised Land are wedded together in the *Am ha'Aretz*. Out of that emerges a renewed understanding of God which the Jews, God bless them, have allowed to slip away too often into abstract intellectualism and legalistic moralism.

It seems clear to me that in the providential care of God the force of divine revelation within his covenant partnership with Israel has been bringing about one of those events in which the potter breaks the earthen vessel because it has become spoiled and unfit for its destined purpose and moulds it all over again. I believe that out of the crucible of Israel's unparalleled sufferings in modern times and out of its living experience in the Holy Land today a much deepened, more embodied understanding of God is emerging from which Christian people and indeed all mankind have something supremely important to learn which they could not learn otherwise. All kinds of issues bearing, for example, upon the pressing ecological and ethical problems of the world today will be affected. But throughout them all there will surely develop a new unitary outlook upon God and the universe in which the physical and the spiritual, the tangible and the intangible, the visible and the invisible, the temporal and the eternal, the natural and the supernatural, the moral and the religious, will be found to interpenetrate and coinhere in each other within the covenant faithfulness of God exhibited in the actual form and shape that it takes in the life and existence of Israel. Thus the original relation between the people, the land and the book promises to reassert itself in a profounder grasp of embodied revelation when the Incarnation of the Word of God in Jesus Christ within the human, physical, intellectual and social structures of human being will be thrust forward into the converging lines of Israel's destiny in a way that will affect the whole human race.

(4) *God's revelation of himself through the medium of Israel has provided mankind with permanent structures of thought and speech about him.*

Permanent structures are not, admittedly, what people today like, not to speak of permanent structures bound up with a people and its culture so different from their own. Now of course we have to reckon here with transient as well as with permanent structures of thought, for there are variable as well as invariable ingredients in all areas of knowledge. Even the Holy Scriptures are characterised by features that have only a time-conditioned significance. Nevertheless there are structures of biblical thought and speech found in the Old Testament which have permanent value, both for the New Testament and for the Christian Church. That is why the Church is built upon the foundation not only of the apostles but of the prophets, and in that order, for the Old Testament Scriptures are now assumed within the orbit of the New Testament, for they provide the New Testament revelation with the basic structures which it used in the articulation of the Gospel, although the structures it derived from Israel were taken up and transformed in Christ. Let us not forget that the Old Testament constituted the Holy Scripture for Jesus and was the only Holy Scripture known to the authors of the New Testament. This implies that only as we are able to appropriate and understand the Old Testament in its mediation of permanent structures of thought, conceptual tools, as I called them earlier, shall we be in a position really to understand Jesus even though we must allow him to fill them with new content and reshape them in mediating his own self-revelation to us through them.

Among these permanent structures let me refer to the Word and Name of God, to revelation, mercy, truth, holiness, to messiah, saviour, to prophet, priest and king, father, son, servant, to covenant, sacrifice, forgiveness, reconciliation, redemption, atonement, and those basic patterns of worship which we find set out in the ancient liturgy or in the Psalms. It was indeed in the course of the Old Testament revelation that nearly all the basic concepts we Christians use were hammered out by the Word of God on the anvil of Israel. They constitute the essential furniture of our knowledge of God even in and through Jesus. If the Word of God had become incarnate among us apart from all that, it could not have been grasped — Jesus himself would have remained a bewildering enigma. It was just because Jesus, born from above as he was, was nevertheless produced through the womb of Israel, mediated to us through the matrix of those conceptual and linguistic patterns, that he could be recognised as Son of God and Saviour and his crucifixion could be interpreted as atoning sacrifice for sin. It was because God mediated his revelation to mankind in that patient, informing way through the history of Israel and within the interpretative framework of its relation with God in salvation and worship, that people were able in that context to know God in Jesus and enter into communion with him, and to proclaim him to the world.

I believe that the inextricable interrelation between God's self-revelation in Jesus and his self-revelation through Israel, and thus the permanent authoritative patterns of understanding which God has forged for us in Israel, require to be re-assessed and appreciated by us today in a much deeper way than ever before. We have tried to understand Jesus within the patterns of our own various cultures so that in the West and the East we have steadily gentilised our image of Jesus. We have tended to abstract Jesus from his setting in the context of Israel and its vicarious mission in regard to divine revelation. Certainly we have taken much from the Old Testament into account, the message of the prophets above all, but in the way we find it convenient to interpret what they say. We take Amos, for example, and all the world loves Amos, but Amos is Israel and the world evidently does not love Israel, so that Amos is inevitably uprooted from Israel and misunderstood. That is to say, we detach patterns of thought from their embodiment in Israel as they presented in the Old Testament Scriptures, or even in the New Testament, and then schematise them to our own culture, a western culture, a black culture, an oriental culture, as the case may be. It is not difficult, as Albert Schweitzer found, to show that, when we seek to interpret Jesus like that within the conditioning of our European culture, we inevitably lose him. In spite of Schweitzer, however, the continued attempt to make Jesus relevant to modern ways of thought has had the effect of obscuring him, for all the time we have been engaged in plastering upon the face of Jesus a mask of different gentile features which prevents us from seeing him and understanding him as he really is, as a Jew — and certainly prevents our brethren the Jews from recognising in this stylised Christ which we equate with 'the historical Jesus' the Messiah whom they are still expecting.

The time has surely come for us to enlist the aid of the Jews in helping us to interpret Jesus as he is actually presented to us in the Jewish Scriptures. We desperately need Jewish eyes to help us see what we cannot see because of our gentile lenses, that is, the culture-conditioned habits of thought and interpretation which we bring to Jesus and which make us read into him the kind of observational images which have played such a dominant role in our literary culture and, until recent decades, in our scientific culture as well. Nowhere, perhaps, do we need the help of Jewish eyes more than in our attempts to interpret the Jesus of the Fourth Gospel, to which scholars keep giving a relatively late date, because of the 'Greek' theological ideas they claim to find in it, whereas in point of fact the Fourth Gospel is probably the most 'Hebraic' book in the New Testament. It was after all in the Fourth Gospel that the evangelist reports Jesus as saying to the half-Jewish woman of Samaria: 'You worship what you do not know; we worship what we do know, for salvation is of the Jews.'

Let me refer to a point of crucial importance where the Jewish mind can help us, in our need to gain a way of thinking of God in which we do not project our creaturely images into God. This is a way of thinking which has been built into the Jewish mind at least from the Mosaic promulgation of the Second Commandment, forbidding Jews to make any kind of image of God, physical or mental. That is to say, through the self-mediation of divine revelation in Israel a way of knowing God was steadily inculcated in which the creaturely images used in its communication such as are carried by the terms 'father' or 'son' were not projected into God, far less the creaturely sex-content of those images. The Hebrew language is replete with vivid dramatic images, for example, in which feminine feelings are applied to God, but the relation between those images and God is an *imageless* relation. The images used are referred to the invisible God imagelessly.

The importance of this way of thinking can be shown from its transference to scientific inquiry, in relativity theory or quantum theory, for example, where we are concerned with objective realities that are quite non-observable, and where we have to decipher the information content of invisible light signals that pervade and illuminate the whole universe. We naturally use English, German, French or some other language, all of which are full of images and figures drawn from the observable world, in our inquiries, so that we have to learn how to use languages of this kind without projecting the images they carry into the realm of invisible space-time, electromagnetic waves, or quarks, for that would be rather a crude mistake. It is significant that at these junctures in modern scientific investigation where we have to penetrate into the invisible intelligible structures that lie behind and control all observable empirical structures in this world, it is very frequently Jewish scientists who have led the way. They have helped us to break through the screen of the phenomenalist world of appearances with which we have become obsessed in our European tradition in science and philosophy. Thus instead of interpreting the invisible in terms of the visible, or the noumenal in terms of the phenomenal, we have had to do the very opposite: interpret what is visible from what is inherently invisible.

That radical change in scientific thought cannot but have a salutary and cleansing effect upon our biblical scholarship and our theological inquiry, where we have to do finally and above all with God who like light is intrinsically invisible, but in whose light we see light. It can help us to take a hard critical look at ourselves in the conflict between our alien presuppositions and the way God has chosen to make himself known through Israel, to appreciate in a new way the permanent value of the structures of thought with which he has provided us in the mediation of that knowledge, and thus help to bring us back to the biblical way of understanding God in the whole field of his activity in creation and redemption, and of course to a way of interpreting the Holy Scriptures without projecting the creaturely content of our conceptual and linguistic images into God.

We have been considering the historical partnership and patient interaction of God with Israel whom he separated from the other peoples of the earth as the medium of his self-revelation to mankind. And we have found that in grace and wisdom God adopted a way of making himself known to his people in which the movement of his revelation fulfilled itself not only from the side of God toward man but from the side of man toward God,and so he brought into being ways of human understanding and human obedience to his revelation which were assumed into union with it and constituted the human expression in concept and word of that revelation in its communication to man. That is to say, divine revelation was progressively mediated to mankind in and through Israel in such a way that it provided a true and faithful human response as part of its achievement for us, to us and in us. Thus there arose in the course of that mediation through the embodiment of revelation in Israel appropriate structures of understanding and articulating the Word of God which were of more than transient value, for under divine inspiration they were assimilated to the human form of the Word of God, essential to its communication and apprehension.

Since all through that progressive movement of revelation the Word of God was pressing for fuller realisation and obedient expression within the life and mind and literature of Israel, the role of Israel as the servant of the Lord in mediating that revelation inevitably pointed ahead of itself to a fulfilment in the Incarnation. When that took place in the birth of Jesus, Son of Mary and Son of God, the whole prehistory of that mediation was gathered up and brought to its consummation in Christ in such a way that while transient, time-conditioned elements fell away, basic, permanent ingredients in God's revelation to Israel were critically and creatively taken up and built into the intelligible framework of God's full and final self-revelation to mankind. Incarnate as the Jew from Bethlehem and Nazareth Jesus Christ stood forth, not only as the controlling centre of the mediation of divine revelation in and through Israel, but as himself the personal *self*-revelation of God to man, the eternal Word of

God made flesh once for all within the objective and subjective structures of human existence. Thus Jesus Christ, not Israel, constitutes the reality and substance of God's self-revelation, but Jesus Christ in Israel and not apart from Israel, so that Israel the servant of the Lord is nevertheless included by God for ever within his elected way of mediating knowledge of himself to the world. Since Israel as a whole is given a permanent place in God's revelation of himself, the Old Testament mediation of revelation must be appreciated and understood from the perspective of its fulfilment in Christ. On the other hand, Jesus Christ is to be recognised and known as Son of God and Saviour of the world, in accordance with his own claims, from the normative framework of basic preconceptions divinely prepared and provided in the Old Testament Scriptures. Thus to detach Jesus from Israel or the Incarnation from its deep roots in the covenant partnership of God with Israel would be a fatal mistake.

As the full and final self-revelation of God, however, Jesus Christ confronts us as One who is identical with the divine Self whom he reveals. That is to say, he is one with the Lord God who proclaimed in his unique self-revelation to Israel: 'I am the Lord your God, You shall have no other gods before me. You shall not make any graven image or likeness of God for yourself.' And so, as St John reports to us, at the end of his ministry as he went forth to consummate on the Cross the supreme act of God's self-giving for mankind, Jesus took into his own mouth the very words of God Almighty: '*I am.*' 'I am the Way, the Truth, and the Life. No one goes to the Father but by me.' He took care to explain that he who has seen him has seen the Father, for the Father dwells in him and he dwells in the Father. What God the Father has revealed of himself in Jesus Christ his Son, he is in himself; and what he is in himself as God the Father he reveals in Jesus Christ the Son. The Father and the Son are One, one in Being and one in Agency. Thus in Jesus Christ the Mediation of divine Revelation and the Person of the Mediator perfectly coincide. In Jesus Christ God has given us a Revelation which is identical with himself. Jesus Christ *is* the Revelation of God.

CHAPTER TWO

The Mediation of Reconciliation

In the last chapter we considered the mediation of Christ in relation to the progressive unfolding of God's self-revelation to mankind in and through the people of Israel. We tried to understand something of the historical ordeal to which Israel was subjected in its adaptation as the covenanted medium of that revelation. To be the chosen partner of God in mediating that revelation was a painful experience for Israel, since the intimate proximity to God which that involved had the effect of stirring up and accentuating within Israel the latent tension in human being between man and God, while the purity of divine truth and love steadily consumed the alien preconceptions which Israel inevitably brought to its reception and understanding of the Word of God. While the stress in our consideration of the mediation of Christ so far has been laid on revelation, we noted that revelation and reconciliation belong together, so that we cannot think out the mediation of revelation apart from the mediation of reconciliation, which is the theme to which this chapter is devoted. The intertwining of reconciliation with revelation is very apparent in God's interaction with Israel, in which a profound reciprocity between God and human being became established in the mind and worship and the very existence of this people.

Here we are in touch with a basic principle of knowledge, which is worth taking time to consider. All genuine knowledge involves a cognitive union of the mind with its object, and calls for the removal of any estrangement or alienation that may obstruct or distort it. This is a principle that applies to all spheres of knowledge, and not simply to our knowledge of God. I have sometimes argued that a person can be a good scientist or mathematician without being morally upright. All of us, I suppose, are aware of scientists or mathematicians who are not morally good people, and perhaps of some who are quite immoral or depraved. A number of years ago, when I ventured to say to a group of scientists, mathematicians and theologians that while an immoral person could be a good mathematician he could not be a good theologian, an eminent mathematician, Professor Gonseth, objected. He insisted that a good mathematician had to be dedicated to integrity and rigour which could not but affect his whole character. In fact he claimed that mathematics induces what he called 'a sanctity of mind'. That was certainly true in his case, and in the case of many others to whom we might refer, not to speak of outstanding people like Pascal, Clerk Maxwell, or Einstein.

Nevertheless, it is largely true that in mathematics, where we are concerned with impersonal or abstract truth, our personal being is relatively unaffected. That is not the case in our relations with other persons which are mutually modifying. In fact we are not really able to know other people except in so far as we enter into reciprocal relations with them through which we ourselves are affected, that is, in friendship. If it is a fundamental principle that we may know something only in accordance with its nature, then we may know it only as we allow its nature to prescribe to us the mode of knowing appropriate to it and to determine for us the way in which we must consciously behave toward it. Personal beings require from us, therefore, personal modes of knowledge and behaviour, that is, the kind of knowledge that comes through a rapprochement or communion of minds characterised by mutual respect, trust and love. It cannot be otherwise with our knowledge of God. If we are really to know God in accordance with his nature as he discloses himself to us, we require to be adapted in our knowing and personal relations toward him — that is why we cannot know God without love, and if we are estranged without being reconciled to him. Knowing God requires cognitive union with him in which our whole being is affected by his love and holiness. It is the pure in heart who see God.

That God may be known only in a godly way, in accordance with his nature as God, is an emphasis that one finds in whole areas of Christian theology, especially in ancient times. I have in mind what is sometimes called the tradition of ascetic theology in the patristic period, where stress was laid upon the need for *askesis* or spiritual discipline in mind and life promoting a way of understanding of God that is worthy of him. To know God and to be holy, to know God and worship, to know God and to be cleansed in mind and soul from anything that may come between people and God, to know God and be committed to him in consecration, love and obedience, go inseparably together. That is to say, ascetic theology sought to put into serious effect the fact that the knowledge and vision of God involve cognitive union with him in accordance with his nature as holy love, in which reconciliation and communion with God through Christ and under the purifying impact of the Holy Spirit are progressively actualised in the renewal and transformation of human patterns of life and thought. The closer people draw near to God, the more integrated their spiritual and physical existence becomes, and the more integrated their spiritual and physical existence becomes, the closer they may draw near to God in mind and being in ways that are worthy of him.

Israel's Partnership with God

That is very like what we find taking place in Israel's partnership with God in which revelation and reconciliation proceeded together throughout the course of its unique mission in history, in which, as we have seen, intensifying conflict and deepening conformity with God were being worked out. The foundations of that covenant partnership between God and his people were clearly expressed by God: 'I am holy: be ye holy.' The unconditional self-giving of God to Israel called for an unconditional response from Israel. Thus Israel became implicated in relations of holiness with God which affected the foundation and character of its existence in the most distinctive and idiosyncratic way as God's 'peculiar people' — that is, the people upon which God has set the mark of his special ownership, the people in whom God 'recorded his Name' through the embodiment of his revealing and reconciling purpose within the very reasons for its existence and continuance among the nations of the earth. Israel was the people which became so intimately locked into the holy presence of God that it was completely spoiled for any naturalistic existence as an ordinary nation, but became the means through which God worked out in the midst of the nations a way of reconciliation with himself in which the tensions embedded in man's alienated existence are resolved and the peace of God is built into the whole of his creation. Israel thus became the people impregnated with the promise of *shalom* for all humankind.

Attention should be focussed upon several features in Israel's relation with God which may help us to probe more deeply into its divine vocation in the mediation of reconciliation as it was brought to its fulfilment in Jesus Christ.

(1) The covenant between God and Israel was not a covenant between God and a holy people, but precisely the reverse. It was a covenant established out of pure grace between God and Israel in its sinful, rebellious and estranged existence. Hence, no matter how rebellious or sinful Israel was, it could not escape from the covenant love and faithfulness of God. That is the aspect of the covenant that is brought out so poignantly in the book of Hosea. Even if Israel persists in adulterating its relationship with God, he will not divorce Israel, for the bonds of God's steadfast love retain their hold upon Israel and lock it into a relationship with God which will finally triumph over all estrangement and bring about reconciliation and peace. There were evidently critical moments in Israel's history when it seemed ready to do anything to flout the will of God in the hope of breaking loose from the grip of his unswerving love and of escaping from the painful transformation of its existence that relations with

'the Holy One of Israel' involved. No, the covenant was not made with a holy people, nor did its validity depend upon a contractual fulfilment of its conditions on the part of Israel, for it was a unilateral covenant which depended for its fulfilment upon the unconditional grace of God and the unrelenting purpose of reconciliation which he had pledged to work out through Israel for all peoples. And therefore, as we shall see in the fourth chapter, it depended upon a vicarious way of response to the love of God which God himself provided within the covenant — a way of response which he set out in the liturgy of atoning sacrifice and which he insisted on translating into the very existence of Israel in its vocation as 'servant of the Lord'. God had, as it were, lassoed Israel by the cords of his covenant love and drew them increasingly tighter as his partnership with Israel held on its reconciling course through history. They were so tightly drawn that already in the Isaianic 'servant songs' 'the Holy One of Israel' and 'the servant of the Lord' were within a hair's breadth of coinciding through the embodiment of reconciliation in the very existence of Israel, which pointed ahead to the Incarnation.

(2) We must turn back again to the fact that the covenant partnership of God with Israel had the effect of intensifying the conflict of Israel with God. So long as the cords of the covenant were not drawn tight, and God remained, so to speak, at a distance, the conflict was not very sharp, but the closer God drew near the more the human self-will of Israel asserted itself in resistance to its divine vocation. Thus the more fully God gave himself to this people, the more he forced it to be what it actually was, what we all are, in the self-willed isolation of fallen humanity from God. Thus the movement of God's reconciling love toward Israel not only revealed Israel's sin but intensified it. That intensification, however, is not to be regarded simply as an accidental result of the covenant but rather as something which God deliberately took into the full design of his reconciling activity, for it was the will and the way of God's grace to effect reconciliation with man at his very worst, precisely in his state of rebellion against God. That is to say, in his marvellous wisdom and

love God worked out in Israel a way of reconciliation which does not depend on the worth of men and women, but makes their very sin in rebellion against him the means by which he binds them for ever to himself and through which he reconstitutes their relations with him in such a way that their true end is fully and perfectly realised in unsullied communion with himself.

That is the way in which we are surely to interpret the Incarnation, in which God has drawn so near to man and drawn man so near to himself in Jesus that they are perfectly at one. In Jesus the problematic presence of God to Israel, the distance of his nearness and the nearness of his distance, which so deeply troubled the soul of psalmists and prophets alike, was brought to its resolution. In Jesus, as the angel announced to the Virgin Mary, there was born none other than *Emmanuel*, 'God with us", that is, the mediator between God and man, who is both God and man in one incarnate Person, in whom and through whom and in the form of whom divine reconciliation is finally accomplished. In this Jesus, however, the Jew in whom the Creator Word and man the creature, the God of the covenant and man the covenanted partner, are brought together, all the interaction of God with Israel throughout history, and all the intensifying conflict of Israel with God, are brought to their supreme culmination, so that from the moment of his birth at Bethlehem the road ran straight to the crucifixion. That was the very point of Simeon's prophecy when he took the infant Jesus into his arms in the Temple: with Jesus the contradiction between man and God was set for its fulfilment, while the heart of his mother would be pierced with a sword. Thus with the Incarnation the conflict between Israel and God would reach its most intense form, when Israel would suffer upheaval and the secrets of its existence would be laid bare. Intense and fearful as that state of affairs would be, it would be but the obverse of the reconciliation that God was bringing to its fulfilment. Hence throughout the earthly life of Jesus the fearful tension he embodied — how he was straitened until it was accomplished — and the reconciling love of God which he incarnated, advanced toward their climax in the crucifixion and resurrection of the Messiah, when all things in Israel and in humanity as a whole, were set within the frame of the new covenant of forgiveness and reconciliation through the body and blood of Christ.

From an outward historical point of view it is evident that Jesus was resented and crucified because he refused to have anything to do with being a national messiah. Thus the tension that developed between the Jews and Jesus was a repetition and an externalisation of the inner conflict, which we considered in the last chapter, between Israel's national aspirations and its vocation as a priestly people, between its ethnic will and its laic destiny. The Jewish authorities, not without popular nationalist support, wanted to invest Jesus with the role of a political messiah in restoring the rule of Israel, which would have conflicted with his reconciling and atoning mission. Right from the start of his public ministry, inaugurated by his Baptism at the hands of John when he was consecrated as the Lamb of God to bear the sins of the world, he had renounced the use of worldly power as a demonic temptation, and chose instead the way of the 'suffering servant' and the Cross. The term 'messiah' had become so identified in the mind of the people of the time with a forceful political figure, that Jesus declined to take it on his lips except at certain moments of critical disclosure in the fulfilment of his revealing and reconciling purpose. He had come, Son of God incarnate as Son of man, in order to get to grips with the powers of darkness and defeat them, but he had been sent to do that not through the manipulation of social, political or economic power-structures, but by striking beneath them all into the ontological depths of Israel's existence where man, and Israel representing all mankind, had become estranged from God, and there within those ontological depths of human being to forge a bond of union and communion between man and God in himself which can never be undone.

Jesus did not come, therefore, to reorganise the human, social and political structures on the surface of Israel's life, which could not touch the forces of evil underlying them but only provide them with a new disposition of structures to use for their own ends, for he knew that those forces of evil are

most deadly when they clothe themselves with the structures of what is right and good. He came, rather, to penetrate
into the innermost existence of Israel in such a way as to
gather up its religious and historical dialogue with God into
himself, to make its partnership and its conflict with God his
own, precisely as they moved to their climax with the Incarnation, and thus in and through Israel to strike at the very
root of evil in the enmity of the human heart to God. He came
to grapple with evil, therefore, at the very point where under
the unrelenting pressure of the self-giving presence and love
of God to mankind it was forced to uncover itself in the
crucifixion of the incarnate Son of God, and then to deal with
it decisively in atoning sacrifice. Thus it is through the
weakness of the man on the Cross and on the ground of
reconciliation wrought out there that God meets, suffers, and
triumphs over the enmity entrenched in human existence
and history and over its distortion of the socio-political
patterns of human life.

This is not, of course, what the world today wants to
believe, any more than Jesus' contemporaries in Israel wanted
to believe it, for the Cross has the effect of emptying the
power-structures that the world loves so much, of their
vaunted force. And so people continue trying to make Jesus
serve their own ends in the world, thereby 'crucifying' him
all over again. Let us be quite frank. Jesus was crucified by the
political theology of his own day, but is that not what people,
even in the Church, continue to do when under a programme
of putting Christian ideals into effect they politicise the role
of Jesus in human society and in international relations
today? The deadly root of man's inhumanity to man, the
source of all human violence, is in the wickedness of the
human heart, and it is there that it must be undone. That is
why God forged in Israel a medium for the Incarnation of his
love, and why he took the meek and lowly way of
incarnational and atoning activity to open up the human
heart to God and ground reconciliation within the depths of
human being. That was the one way of healing and recreating what he had made, when it went wrong.

(3) Now let us consider God's way of reconciliation from

a slightly different angle, taking our basic cue once again from his relations with Israel. Israel was separated from the other peoples of the human race and brought into a partnership of covenant love with God of a unique kind which he unilaterally established and maintained. God threw a circle of reconciling love around Israel, within which Israel was called and formed to be the earthly medium and human counterpart not only of divine revelation but of divine reconciliation. Israel was thus invested with a vicarious mission and function in mediating the covenant purpose of reconciliation and redemption for all mankind. We recall that in the progressive embodiment of his self-revelation to Israel and in his patient remoulding of its existence and life in the service of divine revelation to all men, God became locked in a profound struggle with Israel. The Word of God pressed hard upon Israel throughout its history, informing its worship with the knowledge of the living God and impregnating its way of life with divine truth, thereby evoking obedience but also provoking disobedience, in order to lay hold upon both as the instrument of its ever-deepening penetration into the inner recesses of Israel's being and soul and understanding, thus preparing Israel as the matrix for the Incarnation of the Word in Jesus Christ.

Reconciliation through Israel and in Jesus

So it was also in the mediation of reconciliation. Israel was called by God to be his covenanted *vis à vis* on earth in space and time in the movement of God's love to reconcile all mankind to himself. But that involved God in a passionate struggle with his people, for the embodiment of his steadfast love within its estranged existence, in which Israel persisted in trying to break free from its destiny as the servant of God's reconciling love for all men, had the effect of intensifying Israel's recalcitrance and sharpening the tension between man and God latent in it. In that state of affairs the mediation of divine reconciliation to all mankind in and through the people of Israel could be worked out only in the heart of its conflict with God in such a way that its deep-seated human estrangement from God became the very means used by God in actualising his purpose of love to reconcile the whole world to himself.

Now that is one of the ways of God which we may find rather difficult to appreciate, but look at it in this way. Recall the Evangelist's account of how James and John approached Jesus on his way up to Jerusalem just before his passion when Jesus was to inaugurate his Kingdom. The two disciples asked that they might have the privilege of sitting in state with Jesus, one at his right hand and the other at his left. The other disciples were appalled at the selfishness of James and John in seeking for themselves the first places in the Kingdom, but we do not read that Jesus rebuked them, except to say that they did not understand what they were asking. 'Can you drink the cup that I drink, or be baptised with the baptism that I am baptised with?' he asked. Then when they answered that they could, Jesus promised that they would indeed drink the cup that he drank and he baptised with the baptism with which he was baptised. A short time later he sat down with all the disciples at the passover meal at which he inaugurated the new covenant in his body and blood for the remission of sins, in terms of which the bond between the disciples and himself as the Messiah was knotted in an unforgettable and unbreakable way. Then Jesus was betrayed and crucified, and the disciples found themselves utterly overwhelmed and bewildered at what had taken place, standing in the crowd of those who mocked and jeered at the helplessness of Jesus on the Cross. Jesus was now utterly alone, and they his disciples were separated from him by an unbridgeable chasm of shame and horror for they had all forsaken him and betrayed the very love with which he had bound them to himself. Then the disciples remembered the Holy Supper and Jesus' solemn enactment of the new covenant for the remission of sins in his body and blood. Jesus had meant them to remember, for in that act he had taken their very sins, even their denial of him, as he explicitly showed Peter, and used them as the very means by which to bind them to him. Then the disciples understood the passion of Christ, not as something for the holy but precisely for the

sinner. It was their sin, their betrayal, their shame, their
unworthiness, which became in the inexplicable love of God
the material he laid hold of and turned into the bond that
bound them to the crucified Messiah, to the salvation and
love of God for ever.

It is surely in that light that we must understand the
relation of Jesus to Israel, in its election to be God's covenant
partner in mediating reconciliation to mankind. But in doing
so — and here we must clap our hands upon our mouth and
speak only in fear and trembling within the forgiving love of
God — Israel was elected also to reject the Messiah. If the
covenant partnership of Israel with God meant not only that
the conflict of Israel with God became intensified but was
carried to its supreme point in the fulfilment of the Covenant,
then Israel under God could do no other than refuse the
Messiah. And, as Peter announced on the day of Pentecost,
that is precisely what God had intended, in his determination to deal with our sin at the point of its ultimate denial of
the saving will of God. Recall the question of John Donne
about the Cross of Jesus:[1]

> It bore all other sinnes, but is it fit
> That it should beare the sinne of scorning it?

It is indeed, for that is precisely what the Cross was about.
There the Lamb of God was bearing and bearing away the sin
of the world, including the very sin of scorning it. Thus
within the totality of his atoning and reconciling work, Jesus
took upon himself and made his own all the disobedience
and guilt of Israel, and above all the sin of rejecting him and
handing him over to be crucified. But it was in the bearing of
that very sin that reconciliation was driven into the depth of
Israel's being and nailed there in such a way that Israel has
been bound to God for ever within the embrace of his
reconciling love incarnate in Jesus Christ. That is why the
vicarious mission of Israel in the mediation of reconciliation
to mankind did not cease with the death and resurrection of
Christ but continues to have an essential place throughout all

1. 'The Crosse', Nonesuch Edition, London, 1929, p.288.

history in the reconciliation of the world to God.

It is important for us gentiles, for our own sake and for Israel's sake, to appreciate the continuing role of the Jew in this respect, and the strange, paradoxical nature of that role. If the Jew in his covenant relation to God was blind to the advent of the Messiah in Jesus — and 'Who is blind but my servant?', the prophet overheard God asking — if Israel was blinded in fulfilling its destiny as the servant of the Lord, in the mediation of revelation and reconciliation, then it was blinded for our sake. If the Jew, caught up in man's conflict with God through the vicarious role God has put upon him, could not but react as he did, he was acting in our place and representing our rejection of God's self-giving, so that divine reconciliation might come to us as well and be grounded in the depths of our being. Thus in all our relations with the Jew, we must learn to appreciate that he is what he is for our sake, and that it is through what he has done, even in the rejection of Christ, that reconciliation has come upon us gentiles also. But this means that we may look upon the Jew only in the light of Jesus, the Jew in whom the Son of God became man, and who in gathering up in himself the whole movement of God's reconciling love in and through Israel, gave himself in atoning sacrifice for us and all men. Our indebtedness to the Jew and our faith in Jesus Christ are inextricably woven together in the fulfilled mediation of reconciliation.

It may help us to understand this if we think of it in the light of one of the most profound concepts of sacrifice, in the ancient liturgy of Israel for *Yom Kippur*, the Day of Atonement. On that day the high priest was to take from the community of Israel two goats for a sin-offering and present them before the Lord at the entrance to the sanctuary. One was to be taken inside and slaughtered upon the altar in sacrificial expiation of the sins of the people, including those incurred in their acts of worship. Then the other goat was to be brought forward so that the high priest could lay his hands upon its head and confess over it all the iniquities of Israel and all their acts of rebellion, whereupon it was to be sent away alive into the wilderness, carrying upon itself all the sins of Israel into some waste land. That piece of ritual,

which has ever since haunted the memory of Israel throughout its generations, made it clear that both kinds of sacrifice
were needed to help people understand what God was about
in making atonement for sin.

This does not imply that the ritual acts of sacrifice in the
ancient tabernacle or temple had any power of themselves to
undo iniquity and expiate guilt, for their divinely appointed
function in the liturgy was to bear witness to the fact that
while the holy and living God could not be approached apart
from atoning reconciliation, he himself promised to provide
propitiation for the sin of his people. The fact that the ritual
of sacrifice on the Day of Atonement, when God promised to
renew the covenant which undergirded all Israel's worship,
culminated hidden behind the veil in the holy of holies,
taught Israel that the ultimate ground and rationale of atonement is hidden deep in the mystery of God's own Being into
which it is impossible to intrude. But the rich pattern of
sacrifice and offering instituted in the liturgy gave the minds
of worshippers something definite to lay hold of even though
it pointed far beyond itself to what God alone could do and
would do for his people. That is evidently how the prophet
in the great fifty-third chapter of Isaiah seems to have allowed the pattern of sacrifice, and indeed the two-fold
sacrifice of the Day of Atonement, to provide his mind with
something to grasp, the fact that atoning reconciliation between the Holy One and Israel pressed for its embodiment in
the experience and passion of the servant of the Lord.

In that light, how may we allow the two-fold sacrifice of
Israel's Day of Atonement to reflect for us the significance of
the atoning reconciliation which God has provided and
embodied for us in Jesus Christ? Jesus Christ came from God
and stands before mankind as the Lamb upon whom all our
iniquities and guilt are laid, sacrificed once for all on the altar
of the Cross, but cast out of his own people like an unclean
thing, bearing the penalty of their guilt. We recall that at the
River Jordan Jesus was vicariously baptised into repentance
and consecrated as the Lamb of God to bear and bear away
the sin of the world, and that immediately afterwards he was
driven by the Spirit like a scapegoat into a waste land where

under the burden of our sin he became the prey of the forces of darkness which sought to wrench him away from his mission as the Servant of the Lord. And so throughout his ministry Jesus was held of no account and treated as someone to be avoided, despised and rejected of men. He was oppressed and afflicted, reckoned among the transgressors and cut off out of the land of the living, yet he bore our suffering and was pierced for our transgressions, and he made himself a sacrifice for sin, for the Lord laid upon him the guilt of us all. Thus both forms of sacrifice symbolised in the ancient liturgy were blended together and brought to their fulfilment in the passion of Christ.

The Christian Church went out from the resurrection side of the Cross into history as the Church of the Lamb who had been slain but is for ever triumphantly alive; but the Jewish Church went out from the dark side of the Cross into history as the Church of the scapegoat, cast out and scattered over the earth under the shadow of the crucified Jesus. Each had its distinctive mission to fulfil in bearing witness to the nature of atoning reconciliation provided by God, but each in ways that were the obverse of each other and thus mutely and unknowingly supporting each other. Both participate in the mediation of God's reconciling love through his Servant in whose vicarious passion the Holy One of Israel and the people of Israel, the Redeemer of mankind and mankind itself, are internally bound together. but in one case the perspective is governed by the triumphant vindication of the Servant in which the emphasis falls upon the concept of atonement as a finished work, while in the other case the perspective is governed by the baffling role of the Servant in continuing to bear the disgrace of God's people in which the emphasis falls upon the concept of atonement as divinely prolonged into history, each therefore being directed toward the future advent of the Messiah in a different way.

With the crucifixion of Jesus Christ, and with the overthrow of Jerusalem which seemed, theologically, to follow from it, and with the extension of the Gospel to the gentile world, a schism broke out in the believing people of God which became so deeply entrenched that, after the Bar Cochba

revolt in the early part of the second century, and the dis-
memberment of the state of Israel, the one Church of God
divided sharply into the Christian Church and the Jewish
Church or the Synagogue. As a result of that schism, the
deepest schism in the whole history of God's people since
Christ, both Christianity and Judaism have suffered distortion. In the previous chapter we considered the damage done
to our understanding of Jesus Christ when we detach him
from God's self-revelation to Israel. Now we must reckon
with the fact that schism between the Church and Israel has
damaged our understanding of the atonement. Recall the
long history of Christian theology, Catholic and Evangelical,
and what it has tried to make of the nature of the atonement
thus rendered so problematic as theory after theory was
thrown up, only to prove inadequate, although usually each
has registered some basic aspect of truth. Somehow we are
unable to bring these various aspects together in such a
coherent way that we can grasp the wholeness of the reconciling sacrifice of Christ as it affects the continuation of God's
special covenant partnership with israel and the new universal covenant in the body of Christ through which the Christian Church lives and serves the Gospel throughout the
world.

It seems evident to me that the course of Israel's continued
existence in world history, in spite of all the odds against it,
and the persistence of its mission within mankind, if in a
suppressed form since the crucifixion of Christ, and not least
the re-emergence of Israel in modern times as a manifestation of the Servant of the Lord, have a great deal to teach us.
Certainly the fearful holocaust of six million Jews in the
concentration camps of Europe, in which Israel seems to
have been made a burnt-offering laden with the guilt of
humanity, has begun to open Christian eyes to a new appreciation of the vicarious role of Israel in the mediation of God's
reconciling purpose in the dark underground of conflicting
forces within the human race. Now we see Israel, however,
not just as the scapegoat, thrust out of sight into the despised
ghettos of the nations, bearing in diaspora the reproach of the
Messiah, but Israel drawn into the very heart and centre of

Calvary as never before since the crucifixion of Jesus. The converging lines of its servant mission hidden underneath the spread of Christianity seem to be coming together into focus, gathering up the whole course of Israel's prolonged passion, into a significant pattern. Here the vicarious role of Israel in God's reconciling will for mankind strikes back at us through the shameful despicable implication of 'the Christian West' in the holocaust, prising open our minds to contemplate aspects of the atonement which we have obscured from ourselves but which may prove to constitute the very catalyst we need in our understanding of it.

There are certain profound lessons here which, I believe, Christians and Jews must learn together, each serving the insight of the other before the self-disclosure of God. Let us consider what seems to be involved.

The Vicarious Life and Death of the Mediator

Perhaps the most fundamental truth which we have to learn in the Christian Church, or rather relearn since we have suppressed it, is that the Incarnation was the coming of God to save us in the heart of our *fallen* and *depraved* humanity, where humanity is at its wickedest in its enmity and violence against the reconciling love of God. That is to say, the Incarnation is to be understood as the coming of God to take upon himself our fallen human nature, our actual human existence laden with sin and guilt, our humanity diseased in mind and soul in its estrangement or alienation from the Creator. This is a doctrine found everywhere in the early Church in the first five centuries, expressed again and again in the terms that the whole man had to be assumed by Christ if the whole man was to be saved, that the unassumed is unhealed, or that what God has not taken up in Christ is not saved. The sharp point of those formulations of this truth lay in the fact that it is the alienated *mind* of man that God had laid hold of in Jesus Christ in order to redeem it and effect reconciliation deep within the rational centre of human being.

This was a point that had been stressed by St Paul at the

very beginning of Christian theology. Divine salvation and reconciliation had to do with human beings, not only in the corruption of their physical nature, but in the depravity of their spiritual nature in which they had become alienated and enemies in their minds so that they turned the very truth of God into a lie. Thus the Incarnation had to be understood as the sending of the Son of God in the concrete form of our own sinful nature and as a sacrifice for sin in which he judged sin within that very nature in order to redeem man from his carnal, hostile mind. But St Paul also taught that in the very act of God's incarnational assumption of our fallen human nature he cleansed and sanctified it in Jesus Christ.

That was the doctrine taken up by the Greek Fathers especially, but before long in the fourth century there began a revolt against the idea that Christ took our fallen humanity including our depraved mind upon himself in order to redeem it from within. Thus there developed especially in Latin theology from the fifth century a steadily growing rejection of the fact that it was our alienated, fallen, and sinful humanity that the Holy Son of God assumed, and there was taught instead the idea that it was humanity in its perfect original state that Jesus took over from the Virgin Mary, which of course forced Roman Catholic theology into the strange notion of immaculate conception which divided the Latin from the Greek Church. Strange as it may now seem, Christian theology in the West, not least in so-called 'Protestant Orthodoxy', has largely followed the line of the Roman Catholic Church, although without taking over its notion of immaculate conception — except, interestingly, in a fundamentalist conception of 'verbal inspiration' of the Bible.

If the incarnation is not held to mean that the Son of God penetrated into and appropriated our alienated, fallen, sinful human nature, then atoning and sanctifying reconciliation can be understood only in terms of *external* relations between Jesus Christ and sinners. That is why in Western Christianity the atonement tends to be interpreted almost exclusively in terms of external forensic relations as a judicial transaction in the transference of the penalty for sin from the sinner to the sin-bearer. In the biblical and early patristic tradition, however, as we have seen, the Incarnation and the atonement are internally linked, for atoning expiation and propitiation are worked out in the ontological depths of human being and existence into which the Son of God penetrated as the Son of Mary. The genealogy of Jesus recorded in the Gospel according to St Matthew showed that Jesus was incorporated into a long line of sinners the wickedness of which the Bible does not cover up, but, as we have seen, he made the generations of humanity his very own, summing up in himself our sinful stock, precisely in order to forgive, heal and sanctify it in himself. Thus atoning reconciliation began to be actualised with the conception and birth of Jesus of the Virgin Mary when he identified himself with our fallen and estranged humanity, but that was a movement which Jesus fulfilled throughout the whole course of his sinless life as the obedient Servant of the Lord, in which he subjected what he took from us to the ultimate judgment of God's holy love and brought the healing and redeeming power of God to bear directly upon it in himself. From his birth to his death and resurrection on our behalf he sanctified what he assumed through his own self-consecration as incarnate Son to the Father, and in sanctifying it brought the divine judgment to bear directly upon our human nature both in the holy life he lived and in the holy death he died in atoning and reconciling sacrifice before God. That was a vicarious activity which was brought to its triumphant fulfilment and which received the verdict of the Father's complete approval in the resurrection of Jesus as God's beloved Son from the dead and in the rebirth of our humanity in him.

We shall consider the redemptive and renewing side of that vicarious life, death and resurrection of Jesus more fully in the following chapter, in terms of the way in which Jesus drew the covenant partnership between God and Israel, and between God and humanity as a whole in Israel, into his own relation as incarnate Son to the Father, thereby anchoring it for ever in his own Person as the Mediator. At this point, however, our concern is to recover the awesome truth that through his Incarnation the Son of God appropriated our fallen humanity under the judgment of God. I believe that

God is bringing that truth home to us today as we get a
deeper understanding of the relation of Jesus to the Jews, and
to the Jews in holocaust, where they suffered in the most
abominable way from the emity and anti-semitism accumu-
lated in the generations of Christian Europe. Before that
apocalypse of the abysmal depth of wickedness in the human heart under the pressure of the Gospel itself, we must
understand the Cross as the act of God Almighty taking all
that abominable evil upon himself, through his bond with
Israel fully and unalterably established in Jesus — not by
way of some kind of external transaction but by entering into
it and dealing with it from within its entrenchment in the
depths of perverted human existence.

Now we must surely relate that fact in our minds to the
message conveyed to his disciples by Jesus on the night in
which he was betrayed, that instead of allowing their sin,
fearful and shameful as it was, to separate them from him, he
had laid hold of it as the very means with which in his atoning
sacrifice on the Cross to bind them irrevocably to himself in
the love of God. When we do that, we cannot but think in the
same way of the incalculable crime of humanity in the
holocaust against Israel, and through Israel against God.
Instead of allowing it to shatter the relations of humanity to
himself, God in his immeasurable love has laid hold of it in
order to absorb it in his own passion in the crucifixion of Jesus
and make it through atoning sacrifice for sin to serve the
bond of union he has for ever forged with mankind in Jesus.
But by the same token the terrible holocaust drawn into the
embrace of God's love incarnate in Jesus can be made the
means of Christians and Jews being reconciled to one another in the one mission of mediating divine reconciliation to
mankind. But if that is to take place Jews and Christians need
to help each other in hitherto unthought of ways.

Eli, Eli, lema sabachthani?

We are undoubtedly being forced to rethink the traditional
view of the relation of the Christian Church to the people of
Israel, and are beginning to learn from Jews and with Jews to

interpret the presentation of Jesus in the Gospels in a more faithful way without distorting it through the spectacles of gentile ideas. But how do Jews react to this Christian teaching that in atoning reconciliation God takes upon himself the very thing that separates us from him and turns it into the instrument of his love in binding us to him, when that is applied to the holocaust? Actually our brethren the Jews have been utterly bewildered and stunned by what took place in the concentration camps, overwhelmed by the dark inexplicable horror of 'abandonment' by God.

One day several years ago when I was visiting a kibbutz in Galilee I met a Christian Jewish couple who told me that they were the only believers in the kibbutz for the others were all agnostics or atheists. When I asked why they were unbelievers, I was told that they were all people or children of people who had come out of the concentration camps, and that they had abandoned God because they claimed he had abandoned them in their time of affliction. When I heard that I felt that the terrible cry of Jesus on the Cross was meant for them: *Eli, Eli, lema sabachthani?'* 'My God, my God, why hast thou forsaken me?' That was a cry of utter God-forsakenness, the despairing cry of man in his dereliction which Jesus had made his own, taking it over from the twenty-second Psalm, thereby revealing that he had penetrated into the ultimate horror of great darkness, the abysmal chasm that separates sinful man from God. But there in the depths where we are exposed to the final judgments of God, Jesus converted man's atheistical shout of abandonment and desolation into a prayer of commitment and trust, 'Father unto thy hands I commend my spirit.' The Son and the Father were one and not divided, each dwelling in the other, even in that 'hour and power of darkness' when Jesus was smitten of God and afflicted and pierced for our transgressions. In Jesus God himself descended to the very bottom of our human existence where we are alienated and antagonistic, into the very hell of our godlessness and despair, laying fast hold of us and taking our cursed condition upon himself, in order to embrace us for ever in his reconciling love. He did that in such an incredible way that he pledged his very Being incarnate in

Jesus for us as the immutable ground of our salvation and
peace against all the onslaughts of the forces of evil.

   The inexpressible horror with which Calvary was concerned and the wonder of God's love present in it came home
to me in an unparalleled way in Israel in 1977, when I visited
it as Moderator of the General Assembly of the Church of
Scotland. The Ministry of Religion in Jerusalem could not
have been more kind or helpful. Several of their officials took
me to the Yad Vashem, the holocaust museum, and explained to me its exhibits. I found it an utterly shattering
experience to have vividly and nakedly placarded before me
pictorial and documentary evidence of Israel's indescribable
passion, and of the enormity of the wickedness of mankind
that brought it about. My soul was so overwhelmed in terror
and trembling and my mind so stunned that I could hardly
speak. Finally when we stood together outside and talked
about it, I ventured to ask my Israeli friends how they related
the God in whom they believed so fervently during the Six
Days' War, when they felt that the Lord of Hosts was in the
midst of Israel, with the God of those who perished so
mercilessly in the fires of the holocaust. When they silently
shook their heads and then asked me how I thought of that
relation, I pointed across to the monument erected near the
entrance to the museum and the bronze inscription in Hebrew fixed upon it: 'In your blood, live' — words taken from
the sixteenth chapter of Ezekiel which have been cited
throughout the generations at every act of circumcision. 'By
that monument', I said, 'you are interpreting the holocaust in
terms of the covenant cut into the generations of Israel by the
hand of God, for the blood shed in the holocaust is the blood
of the covenant.' I interpreted that to mean that they were
bound up with God in a covenant relationship in such a way
that they must bring God into the midst of it all as the God
who is afflicted with the affliction of his people, the God who
has not held himself back even from the enormity of the
holocaust. That covenant ceaselessly cut deep into the existence of Israel throughout the centuries gave it a unique
function in history, a vicarious role to fulfil on behalf of
mankind in teaching us all about the living God. Then I went

on and said something like this (I do not recall my precise
words). 'Speaking as a Christian I would say that ultimately
the only answer to your terrible predicament is the Cross of
Jesus which tells us that God has not held himself aloof from
us in our wicked, abominable inhumanity, or from its violence and sin and guilt, but has come into the midst of its
unappeasable hurt and agony and shame, and taken it all
upon himself in order to forgive, and redeem and heal
mankind at the very point where we human beings are at our
worst, thus making our sins the bond by which in atoning
sacrifice we are for ever tied to God.' I had no words from the
Israelis in reply, but as they nodded silently in understanding of what I had tried to say, I knew that we shared together
a deep communion in the love of God which was not far from
the Kingdom of Jesus Christ.

Reconciliation with One Another in Christ

Two days later the Mayor of Jerusalem gave my wife and
myself his best guide to take us round the old city of Jerusalem which was for us a quite unforgettable experience,
although I had often been therebefore. He showed us the
excavations where the Israeli archaeologists were at work
uncovering the underlying structures of several Jerusalems,
and took us round the holy places now opened up as never
before to access by all. Then by design the guide brought us
at the end to the Church of the Holy Sepulchre, and to
Calvary, the spot where, as far as can be determined, or near
which, Jesus was crucified. My wife and I knelt with the other
pilgrims in silence, awe and prayer, while our Israeli guide
stood back a little, waiting. As we came away he took me
aside and said that he could never understand why Christians were divided at that place. I stood rooted to the ground,
appalled and overcome with shame. I do not think I had ever
before realised with such force the blasphemy against the
blood of Christ which we perpetuate by our divisions in the
Christian Church. And the divisions manifested at the Church
of the Holy Sepulchre are quite shocking, for whether the
clergy ministering there are Greeks or Latins, Armenians,
Copts or Ethiopians, they seem to quarrel with one another

in rivalry over matters of privilege and control in such a way that the key to the Church of the Holy Sepulchre has had to be given into the charge of a Muslim. That state of affairs at Calvary indicates the fearful wound which we have inflicted by our divisions upon the Church which is the Body of Christ.

God addressed to me through our Israeli guide a word that is mutely mediated to us everywhere through Jews. How can we Christians claim to proclaim atoning reconciliation through the Cross of Christ when we contradict it by refusing to be reconciled with one another or to allow reconciliation through the body and blood of the Saviour to be translated into our Church divisions? And how can we in that condition bear witness to Jews about Jesus Christ as the Mediator of reconciliation with God, for what we do shouts down what we say? I came away from the Church of the Holy Sepulchre, wondering whether Christians could ever be reconciled with one another without the Jews who have been invested by God with a vicarious role in the mediation of reconciliation to mankind, apart from which even Jesus Christ cannot properly be understood. Quite evidently Jews and Christians must come together in the Messiah, if the world is to be reconciled. Indeed, as St Paul insisted, it is only as Jews and Christians are reunited in Jesus Christ that the fulness of divine reconciliation can be opened to us in such a way that it can be mediated to all mankind. Only when the deepest schism of all is healed in the body of the one people of God and his Christ, will it be possible for the Gospel of the atoning love of God, by which he makes even the wrath of man to praise him, to be proclaimed, to be believed, and to take root in all the peoples and nations of mankind.

God has been making it clear to us in our day, as perhaps never before since the first century, that Israel retains in the purpose of God's grace an essential role in the mediation of reconciliation, and that the Christian Church will not be able to fulfil its own mission in proclaiming that God was in Christ reconciling the world to himself, except in so far as it is incorporated with Israel in the one mission of God's love for all his creatures. That is what the fullness of the mediation of reconciliation in Jesus Christ means.

CHAPTER THREE

The Person of the Mediator

In the first chapter I referred to the problem that results from
the analytical tradition of thought when dichotomous ways
of thinking arise which disrupt and distort the very things we
seek to understand and explain in any field of human inquiry. We isolate things from the matrix of natural relations
to which they belong, abstracting their external pattern from
the ground in which it is embedded and tearing their phenomenal surface from the objective frame which holds it
together, thereby disintegrating them in the very way we
handle them. Then I pointed out the damaging effects of
these ways of thinking upon our understanding of Christ
and his Gospel. They lead to a detachment of Christ from the
context of God's covenant relations with his chosen people,
Israel, to a detachment of Christ from God, and then subsequently to a detachment of the Gospel from Christ or a
detachment of Christianity from the person and work of
Christ. Instead of taking that line, I suggested that the proper
approach would be one in which we consider things in terms
of the actual relations in which they are found, relations
which have to do with what they really are. These are being-
constituting relations or 'onto-relations', as I call them. This
leads to a form of inquiry in which we probe into their
internal relations in order to allow them to disclose to us their
inherent organisation or structure so that we can understand
them in the light of their intrinsic significance or *logos* which
controls our interpretation and description of them.

Let me illustrate this procedure from particle physics. In

classical science we chopped up nature into an infinite number
of tiny entities or particles, the atoms which it was felt could
not be chopped up any further, the ultimate building-blocks
of the universe. But we tried to connect them together in our
understanding through their external relations, that is to say,
in terms of their causally determined interconnections. That
approach certainly had an immense success in allowing us to
throw into strict mathematical form the phenomenal organisation of things when viewed in the large, but it gave rise to the
determinist and mechanistic conception of the universe which
has had such a suffocating effect upon the human spirit. With
that way of thinking in which a hard causalist pattern was
imposed upon nature in detachment from the natural dynamic cohesion of things and events, a radically dualistic
way of thinking infected the whole of our western culture
and led to the widespread disintegration of form so characteristic of the pluralist society and its pursuit of the arts. Now,
however, instead of adopting that atomistic approach, we
have come to think of particles as continuously connected
together in dynamic fields of force where the interrelations
between particles are part of what particles actually are. Thus
we interpret particles not as separated entities but as knots of
energy like tiny vortices in waves of electromagnetic radiation, or as spatio-temporal points of convergence in indivisible
fields of force, in which matter and energy are ultimately to
be equated but which manifest themselves to our 'observations' in split space and time in respect of position and/or
momentum. That is to say, we have come to think of elemen-
tary particles in terms of onto-relational structures in the
space-time configurations of the universe.

   Now it is interesting to note that a way of thinking in terms
of onto-relational structures first developed out of Christian
theology, out of Christology and the doctrine of the Holy
Trinity. This is very evident in the emergence of the concept
of *person*, which was not found before Christianity, for it is
the direct product of the way in which the Church found it
had to understand Jesus Christ and the distinctive relations
in the Triune God as intrinsically personal. Thus there arose
the concept of person, in its supreme sense in God and in its

subordinate sense in human existence, in accordance with which the relations between persons belong to what persons really are in their own beings. That is to say, the relations which persons have with one another as persons are onto-relations, for they are person-constituting relations. That was a concept and a way of thinking developed through the understanding of the Holy Trinity as a Communion of Love in whom Father, Son and Holy Spirit mutually involve and coinhere in one another in the profound onto-relations of that Communion, without any blurring of their hypostatic distinctions or properties as Father, Son and Holy Spirit which would make them no more than modal aspects in an undifferentiated oneness of divine Being.

It is highly significant that it was an onto-relational way of thinking of this kind to which James Clerk Maxwell appealed in the decisive change he initiated in the scientific conception of the structure of the physical universe. Under the regulative force of his Christian beliefs in the nature of God's creative activity as discerned from the perspective of the Incarnation and in the concept of person, he made use of being-constituting relations in his development of a dynamical theory of the electromagnetic field, thereby rejecting a mechanical explanation of it and breaking away from the Newtonian tradition in a mechanistic and deterministic conception of nature. It was from Clerk Maxwell's unification of our understanding of electricity, magnetism and light on this basis and his establishment of the independent reality of the field through his famous equations, that Einstein first crystallised his theory of relativity and went on to bring about the great revolution in modern physics. I refer to this development from Clerk Maxwell to Einstein because when we find a relational way of thinking coming back at us from modern science, it must not be regarded as irrelevant or strange for it has long roots in the history of Christian theology to which, under God, it calls us back.

When we develop a way of inquiry along lines like these and give onto-relations their proper place in our understanding and interpretation of Jesus Christ and his mediatorial work, we are bound to consider them within the dynamic field of God's interaction with Israel in the fulfilment of his purpose of mediating revelation and reconciliation to mankind, for that is the field within which Jesus Christ is actually presented to us. That is what we tried to do in the first two chapters. Now we must turn to consider Jesus Christ in the light of his internal relations in so far as they are disclosed to us, that is, in terms of his own intrinsic significance or Logos. Thus we come to think of him and his work from the knowledge he gives us of himself in his own inner relation to God the Father, and within the constitution of his incarnate Person as Mediator.

The Inner Relation of Christ to the Father

In order to help us see what knowledge of something in the light of its own internal relations means, let me revert for a moment once again to a change that has taken place in scientific knowledge, this time with respect to atomic physics. In classical science the existence of atoms had been postulated, and although no one had ever seen them they were nevertheless taken for granted. And certainly the amazing success of classical physics justified that. However, the more that it was stressed that scientific knowledge of nature is gained only through observations and deductions from observations which in turn had to be verified through correlation with empirically observed reality, the more the question was bound to arise whether atoms really exist. Then under the persistent nagging of David Hume's sceptical questioning of alleged connections in nature that could not be observed, and under the powerful impact of Kant's idea that we know things only as they appear to us, not as they are in themselves or in their internal relations, the matter came to a head in an open debate at the end of the nineteenth century between two well known men of science. Ernst Mach claimed that atoms were no more than 'mental artifices' or 'scientific fictions' needed for the convenient arrangement of observational ideas, which was in line with his conventionalist and positivist notion of science. Max Planck, on the other hand, one of the founders of quantum theory, claimed that atoms were 'real', a claim which was found to be justified by his formulation of a law of radiation in terms of which the absolute magnitude of atoms could be determined, and by his discovery that energy has an atomic structure governed by the universal constant *h*. Before long, however, atomic physicists succeeded in cracking open the atom and knowledge of it steadily advanced empirically and theoretically in terms of its intrinsic connections and nuclear structure. Thus physical science threw off its obsession with an observationalist approach that restricted it to the knowledge of appearances, and developed in a realist direction in which knowledge of things was controlled through the disclosure of things in their internal relations and structures.

Now at last the same kind of change is taking place in theology and must take place if we are to understand Jesus Christ in any realist or authentic way. The investigation of the historical Jesus from the perspective of phenomenalist, observationalist science implies that Jesus cannot be known as he is in himself or in his intrinsic significance, but only as he appears to people, so that the presentation of Jesus in the Gospels is to be understood in terms of what the primitive Christian community made of his appearance to them which they have overlaid with their own theoretical deductions and ideas. By the same token, however, we cannot know that 'appearance' in itself but only as it appears to us, so that it is doubly impossible for us, on those assumptions, to come to any real knowledge of Jesus Christ in his own internal relations. It is hardly astonishing that such an approach to the historical Jesus keeps on losing the historical Jesus!

Now, however, the situation has radically changed, for the assumptions that lie behind that kind of approach and the kind of investigation to which it gave rise have been shattered in the foundations of modern scientific knowledge, so that the way is open for the development of appropriate forms of inquiry in which we allow Jesus to disclose himself to us in the light of his own intrinsic Logos and in terms of his own internal relations. That is the line we adopt here, not because it is in accord with scientific investigations in other fields, but because it is required of us by the very nature of

God's self-revelation to us in Jesus Christ and the way in which through Christ our knowing is reconciled to the truth of what Jesus Christ is in his own incarnate Person. We are nevertheless grateful to natural science for the way in which it has cleared the ground of false notions and exposed damaging preconceptions within which biblical and theological scholarship have too often been trapped, although we cannot enter further into these epistemological or methodological questions here.

Our concern is to offer a theological account of the Person of Christ the Mediator from within the objective frame of meaning which he has created for his Church through his revealing and reconciling activity, that is, within the compass of the Gospel message with which he has clothed himself or within which he has presented himself to us as the Word and Truth of God incarnate. Thus we seek to understand him in accordance with his own intelligibility, in the light of his intrinsic Logos, and in terms of his internal relations in so far as they are disclosed to us, for we may know him truly only out of himself and interpret what we are given to know through modes of thought and speech which are made appropriate to him under the creative impact of his Word and Truth upon us. That is why, when the early Fathers sought to develop their knowledge of Jesus Christ in this way and to give it a clear doctrinal structure in order to defend it from heretical distortion, they found they had to reconstruct the foundations of their knowledge, and remint the basic terms and concepts they used, if they were to become more adequate for this purpose.

It soon became very clear to the Church in those early centuries that the dualist basis of knowledge with which Greek thought operated was particularly troublesome, for it made axiomatic a conceptual outlook in which a sharp distinction was drawn between a divine realm of timeless ideas and an earthly realm of empirical events in space and time. This had the effect, as we can see in the writings of the 'gnostic' sects, of driving a deep wedge between creation and redemption, and correspondingly, between the Old Testament and the New Testament, and of dividing the activity of

God the Creator from the activity of God the Redeemer, which made mythological nonsense of the Incarnation. When this dualist outlook infected the thinking of people within the Christian Church, it was found that they inevitably cut Christ into two, into a divine aspect and into a human aspect. Then in formulating a doctrine of Christ they inevitably started either from his humanity and tried to get across to his divinity or started from his divinity and tried to get across to his humanity. That is to say, in today's terminology, they operated either with a Christology from below, or a Christology from above. The instructive fact that emerged, however, was that each approach ended up by denying itself and passing over into the opposite, so that there was no solution to the problem created by their dualistic thinking of Christ. And so it became clear to the great patristic theologians that a very different, unitary approach to the doctrine of Christ was needed, one in which they understood him right from the start in his wholeness and integrity as one Person who is both God and man. It was only as they allowed Jesus Christ in his whole undivided reality to disclose himself to them as the Mediator, that they were able to formulate a doctrine of Christ which did justice to the whole frame of the Gospel within which and from which he confronted them as Lord and Saviour.

The Oneness in being between the Son and the Father

The basic clue with which those Church theologians worked, as we can see in the Council of Nicaea in the early fourth century, was the Father/Son or Son/Father relationship. They developed this clue through careful exegesis of a host of biblical passages in which they sought to distil the essential heart of the Gospel and the fundamental relations which it involved. One of the most important passages they used was taken from St Matthew 11:27 and St Luke 10:22, which they interpreted along with parallel passages from St John. 'Everything is entrusted to me by my Father; and no one knows the Son but the Father and no one knows the Father but the Son and those to whom the Son may choose to reveal him.' What impressed the Church was the fact that in those

words our Lord spoke of a mutual relation of knowing
between the incarnate Son and God the Father, and in the
Johannine parallels of a mutual relation of knowing and
loving between Jesus Christ and the Father, which implied a
mutual relation of being between the Son and the Father
within which such an exclusive circle of knowing and loving
between them was possible. The Father dwells in the Son and
the Son dwells in the Father in a fully mutual relation of being
and agency upon which the very substance of the Christian
Gospel depends, as we have already had occasion to make
clear in the last chapter.

The supreme point which I wish to stress in this chapter is
the fact that the Father/Son or Son/Father relationship falls
within the very Being of God. That is to say, the Sonship
embodied in Jesus Christ belongs to the inner relations of
God's own eternal Being, so that when Jesus Christ reveals
God the Father to us through himself the only begotten Son,
he gives us access to knowledge of God in some measure as
he is in himself. You and I are children of God, for we are
creatures of God upon whom he lavishes his love and within
whom he dwells through the presence of his Holy Spirit. Our
being children *of* God falls outside the Being of God, for we
are created beings, utterly distinct from the Being of God. But
Jesus Christ is Son *of* God in a unique sense, for he is Son of
God within God, so that what he is and does as Son of the
Father falls within the eternal Being of the Godhead. That is
the doctrine of the Mediator, the doctrine of the incarnate Son
of the Father who is of one and the same being with the
Father, by whom all things were made and who for us and
our salvation became man in Jesus Christ. And it is that
doctrine that constitutes the central point upon which the
whole Nicene Creed turns, and rightly so, for it is at that point
that the very heart of the Gospel of God's revealing and
reconciling purpose comes to its doctrinal expression. Everything hinges upon the fact that he who became incarnate in
Jesus Christ, he who mediates divine revelation and reconciliation to mankind in and through himself, is God of God,
Light of Light, very God of very God — that is to say, Jesus
Christ is to be acknowledged as God in the same sense as the

Father is acknowledged as God, for it is in virtue of his Deity that his saving work as man has its validity.

I do not wish to enter further into that high Nicene Christology, but there are two points implied in it to which I would like to draw attention.

First, knowledge of God the Father and knowledge of Jesus Christ the incarnate Son of the Father arise in us together, not one without the other. We do not know the Father apart from the Son, for there is no Father but the Father of the Son. Nor do we know any Son of God apart from the Father, for there is no Son of God but the Son of the Father. That is why the Creed speaks of one Lord Jesus Christ, the only begotten Son of God, begotten of the Father before all ages, begotten not made, by whom all things were made. Thus we come to know the Son and the Father, the Father and the Son, in one indivisible movement of knowing, for that is a knowledge that is grounded in and governed by the mutual relation in Being which the Father and Son have with one another, and which derives from and is upheld by the mutual relation in knowing which the Father and the Son have with one another. Our knowledge of the Father and the Son, of the Father in the Son and of the Son in the Father, is mediated to us in and through Jesus Christ in such a way that in a profound sense we are given to share in the knowledge which God has of himself within himself as Father and Son or Son and Father, which is part of what is meant by our knowing God through the Spirit of God who is in him and whom he sends to us through the Son. Now it is because we do not know the Father or the Son except through the revealing and reconciling work of Jesus Christ, that our knowledge of the Father and of the Son and of the Holy Spirit is, as it were, a function of our knowledge of Jesus Christ. Because God has revealed himself to us and given himself to us in him, Jesus Christ constitutes in his own incarnate Person the mediating centre of that revelation whereby all our knowledge of God is controlled. It should now be clear that in the nature of the case it is theologically quite improper to contrast a Christology from above and a Christology from below, for our knowledge of God the Father and our knowl-

edge of God the Son perfectly coincide in our knowledge of
the one undivided reality of God's *self*-revelation in the
Person of Jesus Christ, the Mediator.

The Incarnate Constitution of the Mediator

What are we then to think of the Person of the Mediator
himself? Jesus Christ is Mediator in such a way that in his
incarnate Person he embraces both sides of the mediating
relationship. He is God of the nature of God, and man of the
nature of man, in one and the same Person. He is not two
realities, a divine and a human, joined or combined together,
but one Reality who confronts us as he who is both God and
man. We are not to think of Jesus Christ, Athanasius used to
argue, as God in man, for that could be said of a prophet or
a saint, and stops short of what the Incarnation of the Son of
God really was. Rather must we think of Jesus Christ as *God*
coming to us *as man*. Nor must he be interpreted just as the
appearance of God in a human form or in the mode of a
human life, for that also would fall far short of what the
Incarnation really was. The Incarnation means that in Jesus
Christ we have to do with One who is wholly God and yet
with one who is wholly man, but very God of very God
though he is, the Son of God comes to us *as man*. That is an
utterly staggering truth, that God the Creator has come
himself to us as a creature in the world he has made, and yet
remains the Creator; that God the creative and sustaining
Source of all human being has come himself to us as a
particular human being, yet without ceasing to be the divine
Being he eternally is.

In this light we must think of Jesus Christ as the Mediator
of divine revelation and reconciliation in virtue of what he is
in his own personal Identity and Reality. He does not mediate a revelation or a reconciliation that is other than what he
is, as though he were only the agent or instrument of that
mediation to mankind. He embodies what he mediates in
himself, for what he mediates and what he is are one and the
same. He constitutes in his own incarnate Person the content
and the reality of what he mediates in both revelation and

reconciliation. That is why the Bible tells us that Jesus Christ *is* the Word of God, not that he is only the bearer of God's Word, for he is the very Truth of God addressed to us in the form of his personal Being. It is this identity between Mediation and Mediator in Jesus Christ who is God and man in his one indivisible Person that is so supremely important for us to grasp and hold on to, for the very essence of the Gospel is bound up with it. If we let go of that inner constitutive identity between Jesus Christ and God, or between the Person and either the Word or Work of Christ, then our understanding of the Gospel begins to disintegrate and finally collapses altogether.

In order to see what is really at stake in this doctrine of the Mediator, let us make a number of assumptions, and ask what follows from them. Let us suppose that the Son/Father relation does not belong to the inner Being of God but falls outside of it, and is no more in the last analysis than the relation between a creaturely human being and his heavenly Father. Let us suppose that there is no oneness in being between man and God, no hypostatic union between the human and the divine nature, in the Person of Jesus Christ. And so let us suppose that Jesus Christ is not Mediator between man and God in his own being, but is only a created intermediary, only a temporary go-between. What then becomes of the Gospel?

Let us take the forgiveness of sins that lies at the very heart of the evangelical message. When we are told in the gospels that Jesus said to someone, 'My son, my daughter, your sins are forgiven', how are we to understand that? Are the words spoken by Jesus in forgiveness merely the words of a creature, even the best and greatest of creatures? But how can a creature forgive sins? That was the question the Jews asked: 'How can this man forgive sins, for no one can forgive sins but God?' They were right, for as the Old Testament makes clear, really to forgive sin is to undo it, to blot it out as though it had not taken place, but to undo an event like that, to undo the time with which it was bound up, is an utterly stupendous thing which only God himself can do. The point is this. If you cut the bond of being between Jesus Christ and God, then you relegate Jesus Christ entirely to the sphere of creaturely being, in which case his word of forgiveness is merely the word of one creature to another which may express a kindly sentiment but actually does nothing. It is an empty word without any validity that does not accomplish what it promises. But if Jesus Christ really is the Son of God incarnate, if he is one with the very Being of God, then his word of forgiveness on earth is the very Word of God Almighty, a word with ultimate validity, backed up by the Power and Being of God himself, which accomplishes what it promises. Then forgiveness really is forgiveness. But cut the bond of being between Jesus Christ and God, and the bottom falls out of the Gospel of forgiveness.

Now let us turn to the revelation of God in Jesus Christ, and suppose once again that, Son of God though he may be called, Jesus Christ was not in fact of one substance with the Father. What then are we to make of his revelation of God? It would mean that we could not think of God as being in himself what he appears to be in his manifestation toward us in Jesus Christ, but could think of that manifestation as having only some transient symbolical relation to God which was not, however, grounded in the Being or God or substantiated by any real *self*-revelation on his part. It would mean that God is not in his own Being what the Gospel tells us he is toward us in Jesus Christ, or that what he is said to be toward us in the love of Jesus Christ he is not in his own eternal Being as God. That is to say, we could not reckon on any relation of fidelity or trustworthiness between Jesus and the heavenly Father, for if there is no oneness of being or agency between them, Jesus would not be in truth or in reality the *self*-communication or *self*-giving of God to mankind, and in the last resort would have no more value than the embodiment of a myth vainly projected out of man's subjective fantasies into God. If, as we believe, Jesus Christ the incarnate Son and God the Father are one, then he embodies the very self-communication and self-giving of God to mankind and constitutes in his own Person the God-given pledge of its truth and reality. But sever that essential relation between the Son and the Father and the whole ontological substance of divine revelation vanishes.

Where does this essential relation between Jesus Christ and God the Father concern us more than in regard to the love of God? Where would we be if the bond between the love of Jesus and the love of God were cut, which would be the case if there were no oneness of being between them, for God *is* love? To claim that Jesus Christ is not God himself become man for us and our salvation, is equivalent to saying that God does not love us to the uttermost, that he does not love us to the extent of committing himself to becoming man and uniting himself with us in the Incarnation. But if God's love stops short at becoming one with us, what kind of God would that be whose love is limited but some finite Deity and not the Lord God Almighty? If there is no unbreakable bond of being between Jesus Christ and God, then we are left with a dark inscrutable Deity behind the back of Jesus Christ of whom we can only be terrified. If there is no relation of mutual knowing and being and loving between the incarnate Son and the Father, then Jesus Christ does not go bail, as it were, for God, nor does he provide for us any guarantee in what he was or said or did as to what God is like in himself.

Is God really like Jesus?

Here we have to do with a theological principle which is of immense importance in pastoral care. How often people have said to me: 'Will God really turn out to be what we believe him to be in Jesus Christ?' That is a question I have been asked on the battle field by a young man who had barely half an hour to live: 'Is God really like Jesus?' Questions like that which gnaw at the back of people's minds but which they suppress and which come to the surface only in moments of sharp crisis and hurt, tell us of the insidious damage done to people's faith by dualist habits of thought which drive a wedge between Jesus and God. Fearful anxiety arises in the human heart when people cannot connect Jesus up in their faith or understanding with the ultimate Being of God, for then the ultimate Being of God can be to them only a dark, inscrutable, arbitrary Deity whom they inevitably think of with terror for their guilty conscience makes them paint harsh angry streaks upon his face. It is quite different when the face of Jesus is identical with the face of God, when his forgiveness of sin is forgiveness indeed for its promise is made good through the atoning sacrifice of God in Jesus Christ, and when the perfect love of God embodied in him casts out all fear. But all that depends upon the identity between Christ's mediation of divine revelation and reconciliation and his own Personal Being as Mediator.

Let us now pursue a cognate line of thought from the same basic assumption that the Sonship of Christ falls outside the eternal Being of God, but in the form in which that assumption was put forward by the Arian heretics of the fourth century in which they have been followed by many modern liberal thinkers. Suppose that he who became man in Jesus Christ was the first and the supreme being that God made, and that as the Logos or Word of God he is the created intermediary through whom God brought the rest of creation into existence, and through whom in his incarnate form he mediates his love and salvation to mankind. What does such a position imply for our understanding of the Gospel?

By drawing a line of demarcation between the eternal Being of God and Jesus Christ who is the head of the creation, the Arians posited an ultimate dualism between God and this world which ruled out any realist thought of his interaction with human beings in space and time or any direct intervention in their affairs. That had the effect, as we have seen, of emptying revelation of any objective content, of reducing faith to a non-cognitive relation to God, and of making Jesus Christ no more than the tangential point within the world where God touches it only in an external way, so that Jesus Christ becomes only a variable image or changing symbol for the way in which we creatures may think of God. In the nature of the case such an image or symbol is not grounded in or objectively controlled by any reality in God himself. It tells us more about ourselves and the way in which we imaginatively devise our human ideas and project them from a centre deep within ourselves, than it tells us about God who in himself remains essentially beyond any real knowing of him on our part. The main point I wish to pursue, however, is that if Jesus Christ is not the Incarnation of the eternal Son eternally and only-begotten within the Being of God, but constitutes a created and temporal centre entirely outwith the Being of God, then the relation between Jesus Christ and God can be construed only in *moral* terms. It is ultimately not different from that of those who love God and obey his commandments and are said to be 'begotten of God', which is just what we find being said of Jesus in ancient and in modern times. That is an assumption, then, with very far-reaching consequences for our understanding of the Gospel and the essential verities of the Christian Faith, for everything is affected by it.

Quite evidently on this assumption atoning reconciliation can be thought of only as it is externally related to Jesus Christ, because if he is not himself of the very Being of God but is outside of God, then he is not himself our Lord and Saviour, for the only one who can save the fallen creature is God the Creator. If Jesus Christ is only morally related to God himself, then the best he can be is a kind of moral Leader who through his own example in love and righteousness points us to a better moral relationship with the heavenly Father, while the atoning sacrifice made by Jesus Christ on the Cross can be understood only in terms of an external moral relationship, as a demonstration of the love of God or as some kind of judicial transaction between God and Jesus for the sake of mankind. Moreover, if we draw out the consequences of that basic assumption further, we find that the doctrines of the Church and sacraments, and of the Christian life, have all to be understood only in terms of moral relations. The Church then becomes little more than a way of gathering people together on moral grounds or socio-ethical issues, a very human society formed out of individuals who are externally connected with each other through common ideals and a common way of life, while the sacraments are 'means of grace' only in the sense that they help to cement moral relationships and promote Christian patterns of behaviour in brotherly love in response to the Fatherhood of God. I have in fact been describing views of salvation, church, sacraments and a socio-moral way of life, uprooted from or related only in an attenuated way to the evangelical and Christological substance of the Faith, that are characteristic of modern Liberal Protestantism but also of ways of thinking that have affected a host of theologians and churchmen in the Roman Catholic Church in our day as well.

Now if these views are right, then divine salvation does not take place in the ontological depths of human being and reconciliation with God does not penetrate into the underlying structures of human existence, as we have been discussing the way in which God has mediated his revealing and saving purpose for mankind in and through his relations with Israel and above all in the Incarnation of his eternal Son in Jesus Christ. There is then no profound cleansing of the roots of the human conscience through the blood of Christ, no radical transformation or rebirth of human being in him, and no ground for the hope of a creation renewed through the resurrection of Jesus Christ from the dead. If Jesus is proclaimed to mankind as a Saviour or Healer, it can be only as one who fulfils his ministry through external relations and means like a human doctor, a moralist or a social worker. But if Jesus Christ is God the Creator himself become incarnate among us, he saves and heals by opening up the dark, twisted depths of our human being and cleansing, reconciling and recreating us from within the very foundations of our existence.

The Unity of Christ's Person and Work

What are we to think of Jesus Christ, then, as the one Mediator between God and man, *if* we believe, in accordance with what the Gospel proclaims and with what the Church has always confessed, that his filial relation to the Father is grounded in the eternal Being of the Godhead, so that he is very God of very God as well as he who for us men and our salvation came down from heaven, and was incarnate by the Holy Spirit of the Virgin Mary, and was made man? Let me spell out in four different ways what that fundamental truth means for our understanding of the Person and the Work of the Mediator himself.

(1) Since in Jesus Christ God himself has come into our

human being and united our human nature to his own, then atoning reconciliation takes place within the personal Being of the Mediator. In Jesus Christ the Creator Word and Son of God incarnate, his Person and his Work are one. What he does is not something separate from his personal Being and what he is in his own incarnate Person *is* the mighty Act of God's love for our salvation. Christ and his Gospel belong ontologically and inseparably together, for that is what he is, he who brings, actualises and embodies the Gospel of reconciliation between God and man and man and God in his own Person. In him the Incarnation and Atonement are one and inseparable, for atoning reconciliation falls within the incarnate constitution of his Person as Mediator, and it is on that ground and from that source that atoning reconciliation embraces all mankind and is freely available to every person.

I believe it is important for us to ask ourselves today whether we tend to regard atonement for sin as some external transaction between God and man worked out by Jesus, or whether we think of it as having taken place within the Being of the Mediator. That will disclose to us whether we have ultimately taken the line of Arians or the Liberals, or whether we have taken the line of the Nicene Creed and the great Greek Patristic theology to which the whole Church is so deeply indebted for bringing to light and expressing the inner structural connections of the Faith once delivered to the saints. If in Jesus Christ the Son of God became incarnate within our fallen, guilt-laden humanity, then in becoming incarnate he not only took what is ours to make it his, but thereby *really* took upon himself our sin and guilt, our violence and wickedness, so that through his own atoning self-sacrifice and self-consecration he might do away with our evil and heal and sanctify our human nature from within and thus present us to the Father as those who are redeemed and consecrated in and through himself. He did all that precisely as Mediator who brought God and man together in himself, thereby actualising reconciliation and recreating our humanity within the holiness and perfection of his own sinless human life, crucified for our sins and raised again for our justification.

(2) Since in Jesus Christ there became incarnate the very

Son of God whose life and being are eternally grounded in the mutual relation between the Father and the Son, in the communion of love which God himself is in his Being as God, then the mediation of divine reconciliation to mankind in and through Christ means much more than the reconstituting of holy relations between man and God, though it certainly means that. Mediation of reconciliation which takes place within the Person of the Mediator himself means that men and women are savingly reconciled to God by being taken up in and through Christ to share in the inner relations of God's own life and love. It means that the eternal communion of love in God overflows through Jesus Christ into our union with Christ and gathers us up to dwell with God and in God. This is another way of saying that the Incarnation, and the reconciliation that took place within it, fall within the life of God. That is what is implied in the Pauline teaching that Christ, in whom the complete Being of God dwells, dwells in us, so that through a relation of mutual indwelling between Christ and us, we are enfolded within the infinite dimensions of the love of God. The Greek Fathers used to speak of that experience as *theopoiesis* or *theosis* which does not mean 'divinisation', as is so often supposed, but refers to the utterly staggering act of God in which he gives *himself* to us and *adopts us* into the communion of his divine life and love through Jesus Christ and in his one Spirit, yet in such a way that we are not made divine but are preserved in our humanity. That is what constitutes the sustaining inner cohesion of our cognitive union with Christ through faith and the very substance of our personal and corporate union with Christ through the Word and Sacraments, for in Christ our human relations with God, far from being allowed to remain on a merely external basis, are embraced within the Trinitarian relations of God's own Being as Father, Son and Holy Spirit.

(3) Since the relation of the Son to the Father belongs to the union and communion of love which God eternally is in his own Being as Father, Son and Holy Spirit, the Incarnation of the Son in which God gives himself to mankind takes the form of a 'hypostatic union' between divine nature and

human nature in his one Person, which is the immediate
ground for all Christ's mediatorial and reconciling activity in
our human existence. The hypostatic union is grounded in,
derived from and is continuously upheld by what is called
the 'consubstantial communion' within the Holy Trinity,
that is, the mutual indwelling or coinhering of Father, Son
and Holy Spirit as three Persons of one and the same Being
in God. That is a union in which divine nature and human
nature are united in Christ in such a way that there is no
diminishing or impairing of his divine nature and no diminishing or impairing of his human nature.

At the same time this is a union which is projected, as it
were, into the actual conditions of our estranged humanity
where we are in conflict with God, so that the hypostatic
union operates as a reconciling union in which estrangement
is bridged, conflict is eradicated, and human nature taken
from us is brought into perfect sanctifying union with divine
nature in Jesus Christ. Embodied within the deep tensions
and contradictions of our rebellious humanity, the hypostatic union took on the form of a dynamic atoning union
which steadily worked itself out within the structures of
human existence all through the course of our Lord's vicarious earthly life from his birth to his crucifixion and resurrection. Incarnation and atonement were internally and essentially intertwined in all he became for our sake and all he
underwent in paying the price of our redemption. The forces
of darkness did their utmost to divide the Son from the
Father by breaking his trust in God and diverting him from
the way of the Cross, through temptations that were all the
more fearful as they were put to him on the very ground of
his divine Sonship, temptations to which he was subjected
not only in the wilderness immediately after his Baptism or
throughout his earthly ministry, but above all in Gethsemane
and even on the Cross itself. But he resorted resolutely to
prayer in anguished cries and tears and overcame them.
From beginning to end Jesus lived a life of such purity and
integrity, such faithfulness and truth, that his incarnate
Sonship stood the strain imposed upon it by the sin of the
whole world and the Father's judgment upon it. The hypo-

static union of divine and human nature in the oneness of his Person, far from succumbing to the onslaughts of the evil one, triumphed over them all, until through atoning expiation for sin Jesus Christ broke through the ultimate barrier of death and condemnation that separates man from God, and completed his mediation of reconciliation in his resurrection from the grave.

It should now be clear that hypostatic union and atoning union implied and interpenetrated each other in Christ's mediation of reconciliation to mankind. The hypostatic union could not have been actualised within the conditions of our fallen humanity without the removal of sin and guilt through atonement and the sanctification of human nature assumed into union with the divine. On the other hand, atoning union could not have been actualised within the ontological depths of human existence where human beings are alienated from God without the profound penetration into those depths that took place through the Incarnation and the hypostatic union between divine and human nature that it involved. That is what came about in Jesus Christ, the Mediator, in whom atoning union and hypostatic union served each other. Yet it is not atonement that constitutes the goal and end of that integrated movement of reconciliation but union with God in and through Jesus Christ in whom our human nature is not only saved, healed and renewed but lifted up to participate in the very light, life and love of the Holy Trinity.

(4) If atoning reconciliation between man and God is not externally but internally related to Jesus Christ, fulfilled and grounded in his incarnate constitution as Mediator, God and man indivisibly united in his one Person, then the Church of Jesus Christ cannot be thought of as only externally related to him. In the Church of Christ all who are redeemed through the atoning union embodied in him are made to share in his incarnational union with them through his birth, death and resurrection and are incorporated into Christ by the power of his Holy Spirit as living members of his Body, 'the earthly-historical form of his existence' (as Karl Barth has called it) among us. Thus it may be said that the 'objective' union

which we have with Christ through his incarnational assumption of our humanity into himself is 'subjectively' actualised in us through his indwelling Spirit, 'we in Christ' and 'Christ in us' thus complementing and interpenetrating each other. In other words, there takes place a relation of mutual indwelling between Christ and the Church which derives from and is grounded in the mutual indwelling of the Father, the Son and the Holy Spirit in the Holy Trinity.

That 'great mystery', as St Paul described it, of the union between Christ and his Church is primarily and essentially corporate in nature, but it applies to all individual members of his Body who are ingrafted into Christ by Baptism and continue to live in union with him as they feed upon his body and blood in Holy Communion. Since the Church is rooted in the hypostatic and atoning union embodied in the person of the Mediator the description of the Church as the Body of Christ is not a figurative way of speaking of some external moral union between believing people and Jesus Christ, but an expression of the ontological reality of the Church concorporate with Christ himself, who not only mediates reconciliation between man and God but constitutes and embodies it in his own divine-human Reality as Mediator.

The Personalising and Humanising Activity of Christ

We cannot develop the doctrine of the Church further here, but in order to bring out the significance of this ontological relation to the Person of the Mediator for us as human beings, let me draw out its consequences in two kindred ways.

First, Jesus Christ the Mediator is the *personalising Person*. One of the traditional problems in Christology has been how to think of the Incarnation of the Son of God as taking place in Jesus Christ without there being two persons in him, the divine and the human, which would make him schizoid, or without his human person being turned into an empty mask of the divine Person which would make the Incarnation unreal. That is not a problem that should have arisen, for it was thrown up by a false, dualist way of thinking. However, in virtue of the fact that the Person who became incarnate in

Jesus Christ is the Creator Word of God by whom all men are made and in whom they consist, and is therefore the Person from whom all creaturely personal being is derived, the Incarnation must be regarded as creative, personalising activity. As the incarnate Son of God Jesus Christ is Person in his own divine Being, but we are all created persons. He is the personalising Person, and we are personalised persons. Thus, far from depersonalising human being, or overriding the human person, the coming of Jesus Christ has the effect of personalising human being in a profounder way than ever before. With the Incarnation there took place an acute personalising of all God's interaction with us, so that the incarnational union of the Person of the Son with our human nature must be regarded as the most intensive personalising of it that could have taken place. In Jesus Christ we have embodied in our humanity personalising Person and personalised person in one and the same being, in whom the personalised person is brought to its fullest reality. Thus far from being emptied or overpowered by the divine Person, the human person is reinforced and upheld in its indissoluble oneness with the divine.

However, we must not forget at this point that the incarnational union was also an atoning union, in and through which our lost and damned humanity is redeemed, healed and sanctified in Jesus Christ. That means that the broken state of human personal being, resulting from the alienation of humanity from God and the conflict between them that became embedded within its very existence, is brought within the redeeming, healing and sanctifying activity of God in Jesus Christ. The problem with our human personality is that it suffers from a deeply set schizoid condition which regularly, and indeed inevitably, gives rise to insincerity and hypocrisy in us. Through estrangement from the personalising source of our being, the image we present, and wish to present, to others has become detached from what we actually are, so that it becomes a deceptive mask.

Thus we become imprisoned in a self-centred individualism which cuts us off from genuine relations with others, so that the very personal relations in which persons subsist as persons are damaged and twisted. That is the state of affairs in which the personalising Person of the Son of God became incarnate, but, instead of becoming insincere and hypocritical himself, he healed the ontological split in human being through the hypostatic and atoning union which he embodied within it, thereby reintegrating image and reality in and through a human life of perfect sincerity, honesty and integrity in the undivided oneness of his Person as Mediator. It is in this sense also that Jesus Christ is personalising Person, for he redeems us from thraldom to depersonalising forces, repersonalising our human being in relation to himself and to other human beings. But what Christ has done, and continues to do, goes far beyond that, for he anchors our persons immutably in his own Person in God, the generating source of all personal being.

Secondly, Jesus Christ the Mediator is the *humanising Man*. Here we have to reckon with a similar problem to that which we have already noticed, which traditionally crops up in the history of Christology, namely, how to think of God becoming man in Jesus Christ without overwhelming his human nature or damaging its integrity. Once again that is a problem that should not have arisen, for it rests upon a dualist basis of thought in which the divine and the human, the Creator and the creature, the infinite and the finite, are treated as logical opposites and therefore as exclusive of each other. However, since in Jesus Christ there became flesh the very Word of God through whom all human beings are created and without whom no single human being has ever existed, the coming of that Word in Jesus Christ must be regarded as a continuation of God's creation and as the bringing of his creative activity to bear intensively upon what God has already made, thereby reinforcing its creaturely status, and, in our case, its human status. That is partly what is meant by the doctrine of the hypostatic union, in which divine nature and human nature are thought of as being united in the one Person of the incarnate Son, in such a way that they are neither separated from one another nor confounded with one another, and in such a way that neither nature suffers loss or change through relation to the other.

That is to say, in the hypostatic union the human nature of Jesus Christ is taken up, established, secured and anchored for ever in its undiminished integrity in the Son of God.

Here, also, however, we recall that the hypostatic union did not take place apart from the atoning union through which sinful human nature is redeemed, healed and sanctified in Jesus Christ. That means that the corrupt state of human nature, which results from mankind's rebellion against God and the ingrained enmity of human being to God, is brought within the redeeming, healing and sanctifying power of the death and resurrection of Christ. The kind of humanity we know only too well in this world of violence and rampant inhumanity is humanity that has seriously lapsed from what God meant it to be. It has fallen a prey to dehumanising forces which have entrenched themselves within the very structures of human existence so that it cannot escape from them. That is something of which each of us is deeply aware, in that not one of us is or can be the man or the woman he or she ought to be. If there were no gap between what we are and what we ought to be, we would not be aware of moral obligations in the way we are, which means that the kind of moral relations that arise in our fallen humanity belong to the fact that we are not the human beings we ought to be. Thus there has opened up a deep gap in our relations with God and with one another which we cannot bridge. This must be linked up in our thought of it with the schizoid condition of the human personality which we have just noted, and not least with the kind of pretence with which it is regularly bound up. The human heart is so desperately wicked that it cunningly takes advantage of the hiatus between what we are and what we ought to be in order to latch on to the patterns and structures of moral behaviour required of us, so that under the image of what is good and right it masks or even fortifies its evil intentions. Such is the self-deception of our human heart and the depravity of our self-will that we seek to justify ourselves before God and our neighbours by a formal, impersonal fulfilment of the divine law in which we remain untouched in ourselves and uncommitted in our own persons. Yet all the time we are fostering the very process of dehumanisation at work in the depths of our beings and trapping ourselves inescapably in insincere and hypocritical personalities.

That is not a state of affairs, however, beyond the bounds of divine reconciliation. Indeed, it was precisely into the midst of that depraved and dehumanised humanity that the Son of God penetrated by his Incarnation in Jesus Christ, that is, into the very split in our human nature where we are not and cannot be what we ought to be, and where we manipulate moral righteousness in the protection of our selfish ends. Through hypostatic union and atoning union inter-penetrating each other he laid hold of both sides of that split and brought them together in his own Person, removing the sin and guilt which perpetuated the split, reconciling man to God and God to man in such a way that he set the whole moral order upon a new basis. That is the moral order he embodied in himself as the one man who was and is the man he ought to be, without any trace of insincerity or hypocrisy. Through the whole course of his human life Jesus Christ was at work healing, sanctifying and humanising the human nature which he assumed from our fallen, dehumanised state, converting it from its estrangement from the Creator back to is proper relation to him. Thus through hypostatic and atoning union fulfilled within his own incarnate Person as the one Mediator between God and man, Jesus Christ became the humanising Man who constitutes among us the creative source for the humanising of mankind.

Now if from this perspective, in the light of the fact that as the Mediator between God and man Jesus Christ is the personalising Person and the humanising man, we look back at the doctrine of the Church, we may be able to see more clearly why the Church is not merely a society of individuals gathered together on moral grounds and externally connected with one another through common ethical ideals, for there is no way through external organisation to effect the personalising or humanising of people in society or therefore of transforming human social relations. But that is precisely what takes place through the ontological reconciliation with God effected in the Mediation of Christ which binds the

Church to Christ as his Body. Through union and communion with Christ human society may be transmuted into a Christian community in which inter-personal relations are healed and restored in the Person of the Mediator, and in which interrelations between human beings are constantly renewed and sustained through the humanising activity of Christ Jesus, the one Man in whom and through whom as Mediator between God and man they may be reconciled to one another within the ontological and social structures of their existence. Because in Jesus Christ human nature is perfectly and indivisibly united to God the Creator, he constituted in his humanity the ontological source and ground of the being of every man and woman, whether they know him or not, but to those who receive and believe in him he is the One in whom and through whom they may be born anew as sons and daughters of the heavenly Father. The very same message applies to human society, for in virtue of what takes place in the Church through corporate union and communion with Jesus Christ as his Body, the promise of transformation and renewal of all human social structures is held out in the Gospel, when society may at last be transmuted into a community of love centring in and sustained by the personalising and humanising presence of the Mediator.

CHAPTER FOUR

The Mediation of Christ in our Human Response

In one of his books Athanasius spoke of Jesus Christ as exercising a two-fold ministry. 'He ministered the things of God to man and the things of man to God.' That manward and Godward ministry are to be thought of as an inseparable whole in the oneness of our Lord's Person as God and Man, and as continuous throughout all the reconciling movement of his life to its culmination in his vicarious death and resurrection, but also as extending after his ascension into his heavenly intercession as our High Priest and Advocate before the Face of the Father. In our consideration of the Person of the Mediator in the last chapter the stress fell upon the ministry of the incarnate Son of God toward mankind. Now we are to let the stress fall upon the ministry of the incarnate Son of God toward God. It will help us to understand this Godward ministry of Christ if once again we take our initial cue from the Old Testament, through reflecting upon the covenant partnership between God and Israel and the kind of reciprocity which God patiently and compassionately worked out in his historical interaction and dialogue with the people of Israel.

We normally think of the covenant as having two parties, God and Abraham, or God and Israel. And that is certainly in accordance with the Word of God in the institution of the covenant partnership. 'I am the Almighty God; walk before me and be perfect.' 'I will walk among you, and be your God

and you will be my people.' 'I am holy, be you holy.' 'I will
be his Father, and he will be my son.' There is another factor
to be taken into account, however, a middle term between the
polarities of the covenant, God and Abraham, or God and
Israel, namely *a covenanted way of response*, such as a divinely
provided sacrifice replacing the best that the human partner
may think he can offer, as in the paradigm case of the offering
God provided instead of Isaac, Abraham's beloved son. The
pattern became very clear in the grounding of the covenant
between God and Israel at Mt Sinai. He knew that Israel
would not be able to fulfil the covenant provisions, that Israel
could not walk before him and be perfect, be holy as God was
holy. Nor would Israel be able to draw near to God and
worship him as it ought. Hence within the covenant which,
as we have seen, God established and maintained with his
people in a unilateral way, and as part of its sheer grace, he
freely provided them with a covenanted way of responding
to him, a vicarious way in which the covenant might be
fulfilled in their midst and on their behalf, so that Israel could
come before God forgiven and sanctified in their covenant
partnership with him and be consecrated for their priestly
mission in the world.

This remarkable feature of the covenant was elaborately
presented in the ordinances of worship that are described in
the Pentateuch. Not only the general pattern of the cult but
the details of the liturgy were clearly designed to bring home
to the people of Israel that they were not to appear before the
Face of God with offerings embodying their own self-expres-
sion or representing their own naturalistic desires, or with
kinds of sacrifice thought up by themselves as means of
expiating guilt or propitiating God, for that was how the
heathen engaged in worship, as ways of acting upon God
and inducing his favour. Thus no unprescribed oblation, no
uncovenanted offering, no strange fire, no incense of their
own recipe, and no ritual of their own inventing, were to be
intruded into their worship of God. Everything about the
sanctuary and everything that was prescribed to be done
within it as the place where God had recorded his name, the
holy place of meeting and witness between God and his

covenanted people, was designed to testify to the fact that God alone can expiate guilt, forgive sin and bring about propitiation between himself and his people Israel. Hence the very priesthood itself, the sacrifices, offerings and oblations which the priests alone were consecrated to take in their hands, together with all the liturgical ordinances, were regarded as constituting the vicarious way of covenant response in faith, obedience and worship which God had freely provided for Israel out of his steadfast love.

The institution within Israel's peculiar relations with God of this divinely inspired cult as its way of liturgical witness to God's revealing and reconciling purpose, once for all set forth in the Torah and steadily interpreted by the prophets, had the effect of reinforcing Israel's separation from the other nations of mankind as a people imprinted with a priestly character and invested with a vicarious mission. It was not good enough, however, for Israel formally to engage in the prescribed ordinances of worship, far less to rely upon God's gift of sanctuary, priesthood and liturgy as guarantees of immunity from divine judgment upon its way of behaviour, apart from obedience to the Word and Truth of God, for by its very nature the covenant envisaged that God's laws would be put into the minds and written on the hearts of his people. That is to say, the covenanted way of response had to be worked into the very flesh and blood of Israel's existence. It had to be impregnated in its understanding and sculptured into its very being. It had to be built into the reciprocity between God and Israel and be allowed to control the whole pattern of its life and mission in history.

An embodiment and mediation of the covenant along these lines governed the profound Old Testament conception of 'the servant of the Lord'. In the Isaianic prophecies particularly the mediatorial and priestly figures of Moses and Aaron and the notions of guilt-bearer and sacrifice for sin were conflated to provide the interpretative clue for the intercessory and vicarious role of the servant in the redemption of God's people. The servant of the Lord was the hypostatised actualisation within the flesh and blood existence of Israel of the divinely provided way of covenant response set forth in the cult, which indicated rather more than it could express. A messianic role was evidently envisaged for the servant in which mediator and sacrifice, priest and victim were combined in a form that was at once representative and substitutionary, corporate and individual, in its fulfilment. As the prophet struggled to bring his vision into focus something emerged which is rather startling. Time and again he spoke about the *ebed Jahweh*, the servant of the Lord who is identified with Israel, and about the *goel*, the Redeemer who is the Holy One of Israel, in the same breath. Thus the servant of the Lord and the Redeemer, the Holy One of Israel, were brought together in his prophetic utterance, and yet held apart but only by a hair's breadth, so to speak. It is as though the prophet wanted to say that the real servant of the Lord is the Lord himself who as *goel*-Redeemer has bound himself up in such a tight bond of covenant kinship with Israel that he has taken upon himself Israel's afflicted existence and made it his own in order to redeem Israel. Now of course if the servant of the Lord and the Holy One of Israel had been identified, that would have implied a state of incarnation, but the Gospel of the Old Testament, as the second Isaiah is sometimes called, could only hold them closely together without actually identifying them.

When we turn to the pages of the New Testament, however, we find that Jesus Christ was recognised and presented both as the Servant of the Lord and as the divine Redeemer who had come to bear and bear away the iniquities, transgressions and guilt of his people, and yet not of Israel only but of the whole world. That was an identification which was regarded as of the very essence of the Gospel. As the incarnate Son of the Father Jesus Christ had been sent to fulfil all righteousness both as priest and as victim, who through his one self-offering in atonement for sin has mediated a new covenant of universal range in which he presents us to his Father as those whom he has redeemed, sanctified and perfected for ever in himself. In other words, Jesus Christ constitutes in his own self-consecrated humanity the fulfilment of the vicarious way of human response to God promised under the old covenant, but now on the ground of his atoning self-sacrifice once for all offered this is a vicarious way of response which is available for all mankind.

It is surely in that light that we are to understand the twofold ministry of Jesus, from God to man and from man to God. In biblical language, he fulfilled the covenant from both sides: 'I will be your God, and you will be my people.' 'I am holy, be you holy.' 'I will be your Father and you will be my son.' Our immediate concern in this chapter is with the fulfilment of that covenant in the body and blood of Christ, from the side of human beings toward God the Father as the divinely provided counterpart to God's unconditional self-giving to mankind. There are, then, three factors to be taken into account, God and mankind, or God and his people, the two parties of the covenant partnership, but within that polarity, the all-important middle factor, *the vicarious humanity of Jesus.*

In this light we must take a further look at the mediation of revelation and reconciliation.

Revelation

We recall that in his historical dialogue with Israel God chose to reveal himself and actualize that self-revelation to mankind in such a way that Israel the immediate receiver would be moulded and shaped into an appropriate vessel for its communication to all peoples. Throughout all the vicissitudes of Israel's national, social and religious existence the Word of God came to israel, mediated through servants of the Lord like Moses, Elijah, Jeremiah, sometimes like a refining fire, sometimes like a hammer breaking the rocks in pieces, sometimes as a still small voice, but always in such a way that the holy presence of God himself in his Word imprinted his truth upon the innermost being of this people with the result that all its relations with God were intensified in obedience and disobedience, in faithfulness and unfaithfulness alike. Throughout that persistent and progressive reciprocity which God maintained between himself and Israel, the Word of God addressed to Israel did not return to him fruitless without accomplishing his purpose or succeeding in the task he gave it. For it laid hold upon the mind and will of this people in a creative way which called forth from it responses that were taken up, purified and assimilated to the

Word of God as the means of its ever-deepening penetration
into the understanding, life and service of Israel, so that it could
be bearer of divine revelation for all mankind.

   That was the movement of God's self-revelation which was
brought to its culmination in Jesus Christ through the Incarnation when the Word of God actualised itself within Israel and
within mankind in the visible, tangible form of a particular
human being who embodied in himself the personal address
of God's Word to man and the personal response of man to
God's Word. In Jesus the Word of God was translated into the
form of a human life in whom there was only truth and light
and no darkness, the Word of Life to be known and grasped
through communion with him, but in Jesus there was provided for mankind a way of response to God which issued out
of the depths of its existence and as its very own and in which
each human being was free to share through communion with
Jesus. Thus in Jesus the final response of man toward God was
taken up, purified through his atoning self-consecration on
our behalf, and incorporated into the Word of God as his
complete self-communication to mankind, but also as the
covenanted way of vicarious response to God which avails for
all of us and in which we all may share through the Spirit of
Jesus Christ which he freely gives us.

   The implications of this fact are immense, some of which
we shall consider later, but at this point let us note this one:
that *the real text* of New Testament revelation is *the humanity
of Jesus*. As we read the Old Testament and read the New
Testament and listen to the Word of God, the real text is not
documents of the Pentateuch, the Psalms or the Prophets or
the documents of the Gospels and the Epistles, but in and
through them all the Word of God struggling with rebellious
human existence in Israel on the way to becoming incarnate,
and then that Word translated into the flesh and blood and
mind and life of a human being in Jesus, in whom we have
both the Word of God become man and the perfect response
of man to God offered on our behalf. As the real text of God's
Word addressed to us, Jesus is also the real text of our
address to God. We have no speech or language with which
to address God but the speech and language called Jesus

Christ. In him our humanity, our human understanding, our human word are taken up, purified and sanctified, and addressed to God the Father for us as our very own — and that is the word of man with which God is well pleased.

Reconciliation

If the covenant promise of God ran: 'I will be to him a Father, and he will be my son', it was primarily in terms of the Father/Son and Son/Father relationship that reconciliation between God and man and man and God was held to be fulfilled. With the Incarnation the Sonship of the Son of God has been incorporated into the inter-personal and family structures of our human existence. In Jesus Christ the Son of the Father has personally entered into our human existence where we have forfeited our right as children of God, inter-penetrated the structures of our personal and interpersonal being-constituting relations as sons and daughters in the creaturely family of God which we have polluted and falsified, twisting them round into their opposite so that instead of expressing genuine filial relation to the heavenly Father they express what we are in our self-centred alienation from him and from one another, thus turning the truth of the very image of God in which we have been created into a lie. But having entered into and made his own that estranged and disobedient condition of our human being, he has converted it back in his own human being in love and obedience to the Father. As we have already had occasion to see, that was a reconciliation which Jesus Christ achieved for us throughout the whole course of his obedience as the Servant-Son and supremely in his atoning sacrifice on the Cross. There he penetrated to the utmost extremity of our self-alienating flight from God where we are trapped in death, and turned everything round so that out of the fearful depths of our darkness and dereliction we may cry with him, 'Our Father'. What he did for us in his own anguished experience of spirit we are allowed to overhear when in Gethsemane he wrestled with God over the cup he had been given to drink: 'Father, if it be thy will, take this cup away from me. Yet not my will but thine be done.' 'Not my will...', that is, your will and my will, our human self-will, which Jesus appropriated and bent back in the agony of Gethsemane in total obedience to the will of the Father, and then acted it out to the end on the Cross. The answer of the Father was given in unmistakable terms in the resurrection of Jesus Christ from the dead: 'Thou art my beloved Son in whom I am well pleased.'

We are to think of the whole life and activity of Jesus from the cradle to the grave as constituting the vicarious human response to himself which God has freely and unconditionally provided for us. That is not an answer to God which he has given to us through some kind of transaction external to us or over our heads, as it were, but rather one which he has made to issue out of the depths of our human being and life as our own. Nor is it an answer in word only but in deed, not by way of an exemplary event which we may follow but which has no more than symbolical significance, but by way of a final answer to God actualized in the flesh and blood of our human existence and behaviour and which remains eternally valid. Jesus Christ *is* our human response to God. Thus we appear before God and are accepted by him as those who are inseparably united to Jesus Christ our great High Priest in his eternal self-presentation to the Father.

The radical nature of Jesus' mediation of our human response to God can be made apparent by bringing together and thinking into each other the concepts of representation and substitution. It will not do to think of what Christ has done for us only in terms of representation, for that would imply that Jesus represents, or stands for, *our* response, that he is the leader of humanity in humanity's act of response to God. On the other hand, if Jesus is a substitute in detachment from us, who simply acts in our stead in an external, formal or forensic way, then his response has no ontological bearing upon us but is an empty transaction over our heads. A merely representative or a merely substitutionary concept of vicarious mediation is bereft of any actual saving significance. But if representation and substitution are combined and allowed to interpenetrate each other within the incarnational union of the Son of God with us in which he has actually taken our sin and guilt upon his own being, then we may have a profounder and truer grasp of the vicarious humanity in the mediatorship of Christ, as one in which he acts in our place, in our stead, on our behalf but out of the ontological depths of our actual human being.

The critical significance of the vicarious humanity of Christ for an adequate grasp of his mediation can be brought home to us by noting how Liberals and Fundamentalists react to the concept of substitution. Liberal theology tends to reject the concept of substitution with contempt, and concentrates upon the historical Jesus, but, as we noted earlier, it regularly tends to lose the humanity of Jesus for what is important for it is not Jesus himself but what he symbolises. Fundamentalist theology, on the other hand, readily accepts the idea of substitution, and concentrates upon the saving work of God in Jesus Christ, and again tends to lose the humanity of Jesus for the Incarnation is regarded as merely instrumental and not internally related to atonement. Both Liberals and Fundamentalists, however, react with a kind of shock when the humanity of Jesus and substitution are linked together for they have not a little difficulty with the idea that it is *as man* that Jesus Christ takes our place, acts on our behalf and in our stead, and that it is precisely *as man* that God himself comes to us in the Incarnation. It is at this very point that the Gospel seems to hurt most, for it cuts like a two-edged sword into our preconceived ideas.

Now for the rest of this chapter, let us spell out something of what the vicarious humanity of Jesus means in the mediation of our human response to God in respect of what we do in faith, conversion, and worship, in the celebration of the sacraments, and in evangelism.

(1) *Faith*

We are accustomed to think of faith as something we have or as an act in which we engage, and of believing as our activity. And that of course would be right, not least in view of the summons of the Gospel to repent and believe, that we may be saved, or of the words of our Lord when he said to people that their faith had saved them or chided others for their lack of faith. But we would be misconstruing that if we thought of faith or belief as an autonomous, independent act which we do from a base in ourselves, for the biblical conception of faith is rather different. Faith has to do with the reciprocity, and indeed the community of reciprocity, between God and man, that is, with the polarity between the faithfulness of God and the answering faithfulness of man. Within the covenant relationship of steadfast love and truth, the covenant faithfulness of God surrounds and upholds the faltering response of his people. As we noted with a glance at the book of the prophet Hosea, Israel was regarded as encircled and grasped by the faithful love of God who will not let his people go, but holds on to them throughout all their rebellion and unfaithfulness until he has called forth an answering faithfulness that is steadfast and true reflecting his own. That is the undergirding and utterly invariant faithfulness of God revealed through his covenant partnership with Israel, upon which all their redemption rests, as the divinely prescribed pattern of Israel's worship constantly testified. It was within the embrace of that faithfulness that God evoked and nourished the faith of individual members of the covenant people as the books of Job and the Psalms above all make clear.

The New Testament concept of faith is not different from that, although owing to the Incarnation it has an intensely personalised character. We must think of Jesus as stepping into the relation between the faithfulness of God and the actual unfaithfulness of human beings, actualising the faithfulness of God and restoring the faithfulness human beings by grounding it in the incarnate medium of his own faithfulness so that it answers perfectly to the divine faithfulness. Thus Jesus steps into the actual situation where we are summoned to have faith in God, to believe and trust in him, and he acts in our place and in our stead from within the depths of our unfaithfulness and provides us freely with a faithfulness in which we may share. He does that as Mediator between God and man, yet precisely *as man* united to us and taking our place at every point where we human beings act as human beings and are called to have faith in the Father, to believe in him and trust him. That is to say, if we think of belief, trust or faith as forms of human activity before God, then we must think of Jesus Christ as believing, trusting and having faith in God the Father on our behalf and in our place.

Admittedly, this is a matter which many people, especially in our Western culture with its stress upon the integrity and freedom of the individual person, find it rather difficult to accept at its face value, for they automatically tend to reinterpret it in line with their axiomatic assumptions — for example, in the stress upon what many people call 'believer's baptism'. Many years ago I recall thinking of the marvellous way in which our human faith is implicated in the faith of Jesus Christ and grasped by his faithfulness, when I was teaching my little daughter to walk. I can still feel her tiny fingers gripping my hand as tightly as she could. She did not rely upon her feeble grasp of my hand but upon my strong grasp of her hand which enfolded her grasp of mine within it. That is surely how God's faithfulness actualised in Jesus Christ has hold of our weak and faltering faith and holds it securely in his hand. Listen again to the words of our Lord's parable. 'My own sheep listen to my voice; and I know them and they follow me. I give unto them eternal life and they shall never perish; no one shall snatch them from my hand. My Father who has given them to me is greater than all and no one can snatch them out of my Father's hand. My Father and I are one.'

We can see how that operates by looking at the relation of Peter to Jesus who held on to him and would not let him go in spite of his unfaithfulness. You will recall how, in the course of that meal in which Jesus inaugurated with his disciples the new covenant in his body and blood for the remission of sins, he told Peter that he would deny him three times, and then added: 'I have prayed for you that your faith may not fail.' Now of course it did fail, but all through that fearful failure it was restored, stabilised and strengthened within the embrace of the unswerving faithfulness of Jesus. It was upon that rock of faith that the Church was built.

Thus in the teaching of the New Testament as well as in that of the Old Testament people's faith is held to have its proper place within the polar relationship between God and mankind. But in the Gospel that polar relation has been

actualised in such a way that we are yoked together with
Jesus in his bearing of our burden and are made to share in
the almighty strength and immutability of his vicarious faith
and faithfulness on our behalf. Through his incarnational
and atoning union with us our faith is implicated in his faith,
and through that implication, far from being depersonalised
or dehumanised, it is made to issue freely and spontaneously
out of our own human life before God. Regarded merely in
itself, however, as Calvin used to say, faith is an empty
vessel, for in faith it is upon the faithfulness of Christ that we
rest and even the way in which we rest on him is sustained
and undergirded by his unfailing faithfulness. Thus the very
faith which we confess is the faith of Christ Jesus who loved
us and gave himself for us in a life and death of utter trust and
belief in God the Father. Our faith is altogether grounded in
him who is 'the author and finisher of our faith', on whom
faith depends from start to finish.

(2) *Conversion*

The Gospel tells us to repent and believe, to take up the cross
and follow Christ, or, as we say, to make our personal
decision for Christ as our Lord and Saviour. That is something that each of us must do, for no other human being can
substitute for us in that ultimate act of man in answer to God
— no other, that is, except Jesus. If we do not allow him to
substitute for us at that point, we make his atoning substitution for us something that is partial and not total, which
would finally empty it of saving significance. Let us consider
again the incarnate life and activity of Jesus which we found
to be atoning activity from beginning to end, and look at it in
the light of his parable of the prodigal son. What Jesus did
was to make himself one with us in our estranged humanity
when it was running away into the far country, farther and
farther away from the Father, but through his union with it
he changed it in himself, reversed its direction and converted
it back in obedience and faith and love to God the Father. The
Gospel tells us that at his Baptism Jesus was baptised 'into
repentance' (*eis metanoian*), for as the Lamb of God come to
bear our sins he fulfilled that mission not in some merely

superficially forensic way, though of course profound forensic elements were involved, but in a way in which he bore our sin and guilt upon his very soul which he made an offering for sin. That is to say, the Baptism with which he was baptised was a Baptism of vicarious repentance for us which he brought to its completion on the Cross where he was stricken and smitten of God for our sakes, by whose stripes we are healed. He had laid hold of us even in the depths of our human soul and mind where we are alienated from God and are at enmity with him, and altered them from within and from below in radical and complete *metanoia*, a repentant restructuring of our carnal mind, as St Paul called it, and a converting of it into a spiritual mind. As fallen human beings, we are quite unable through our own free-will to escape from our self-will for our free-will is our self-will. Likewise sin has been so ingrained into our minds that we are unable to repent and have to repent even of the kind of repentance we bring before God. But Jesus Christ laid hold of us even there in our sinful repentance and turned everything round through his holy vicarious repentance, when he bore not just upon his body but upon his human mind and soul the righteous judgments of God and resurrected our human nature in the integrity of his body, mind and soul from the grave. Thus as the firstborn of every creature he became the firstborn from the dead, and the head of the Church of the firstborn.

It is significant that the New Testament does not use the term regeneration (*paliggenesia*), as so often modern evangelical theology does, for what goes on in the human heart. It is used only of the great regeneration that took place in and through the Incarnation and of the final transformation of the world when Jesus Christ will come again to judge the quick and the dead and make all things new. That is to say, the Gospel speaks of regeneration as wholly bound up with Jesus Christ himself.

During my first week of office as Moderator of the General Assembly of the Church of Scotland when I presided at the Assembly's Gaelic Service, a highlander asked me whether I was born again, and when I replied in the affirmative he

asked when I had been born again. I still recall his face when
I told him that I had been born again when Jesus Christ was
born of the Virgin Mary and rose again from the virgin tomb,
the first-born from the dead. When he asked me to explain I
said: 'This Tom Torrance you see is full of corruption, but the
real Tom Torrance is hid with Christ in God and will be
revealed only when Jesus Christ comes again. He took my
corrupt humanity in his Incarnation, sanctified, cleansed
and redeemed it, giving it new birth, in his death and
resurrection.' In other words, our new birth, our regeneration, our conversion, are what has taken place in Jesus Christ
himself, so that when we speak of our conversion or our
regeneration we are referring to our sharing in the conversion or regeneration of our humanity brought about by Jesus
in and through himself for our sake. In a profound and
proper sense, therefore, we must speak of Jesus Christ as
constituting in himself the very substance of our conversion,
so that we must think of him as taking our place even in our
acts of repentance and personal decision, for without him all
so-called repentance and conversion are empty. Since a
conversion in that truly evangelical sense is a turning away
from ourselves to Christ, it calls for a conversion from our in-
turned notions of conversion to one which is grounded and
sustained in Christ Jesus himself.

(3) *Worship*

Here we keep in mind the initial clue which we took from the
nature and pattern of worship in the institution of the covenant between God and Israel at Mt Sinai. The immediate
pattern of the liturgy, and even of the construction of the
Tabernacle in which the high priest had to ascend from the
holy place to the holy of holies in annual atoning renewal of
the covenant, seems to have been connected with the actual
event of mediation between God and Israel effected by
Moses in his ascent of Mt Sinai, his intercession on behalf of
Israel, and his bringing back to Israel of the peace or *shalom*
of God. But, as we noted, all that was interpreted in the form
of liturgical witness to God's saving and propitiating work,
so that it was made to point far ahead to a future messianic

fulfilment through the servant of the Lord who would mediate a new covenant in which the relations between God and his people would be set on a new and final basis. With its actual fulfilment in the incarnate life and self-offering of the Son of God, Jesus Christ embodied in himself in a vicarious form the response of human beings to God, so that all their worship and prayer to God henceforth became grounded and centred in him. In short, Jesus Christ in his own self-oblation to the Father *is* our worship and prayer in an acutely personalised form, so that it is only through him and with him and in him that we may draw near to God with the hands of our faith filled with no other offering but that which he has made on our behalf and in our place once and for all.

In that perspective we must think of prayer as taking place within the relations of covenant partnership and reciprocity between God and mankind, but of Christian prayer as grounded in and governed by the fact that through his Incarnation Jesus Christ has stepped into that relationship as the Mediator, who not only brings God and man and man and God near to each other in propitiation but who in doing so stands in our place where we cry in prayer to God and makes himself our prayer, a prayer not in word or even in an act only but a prayer which he is in his own personal Being. Just as in Jesus Christ God addresses his word to us in such a way that he himself is wrapped up in his word in the form of personal being, so in Jesus Christ God has provided us with prayer that is identical with the personal self-offering and self-oblation of Jesus Christ to the Father on our behalf. It is as such that Jesus Christ stands in our place where we pray to the Father, so that from deep within our humanity, where he has united himself to us, and from out of it, assimilated to his own self-consecration to God, he prays: 'Our father who art in heaven. Hallowed by thy Name. Thy Kingdom come. Thy will be done on earth as it is in heaven ...' That is to say, where we are unable to pray to the Father as we ought or in any way worthy of him for all our prayers are unclean, Jesus Christ puts his prayer, prayed with us to the Father, into our unclean mouth that we may pray through him and with him and in him to the Father, and be received by the Father in him: 'Thou art my beloved Son in whom I am well pleased.'

We do not come before God, then, worshipping him and praying to him in our own name, or in our own significance, but in the name and significance of Jesus Christ alone, for worship and prayer are not ways in which we express ourselves but ways in which we hold up before the Father his beloved Son, take refuge in his atoning sacrifice, and make that our only plea.

'Nothing in my hands I bring;
Simply to thy Cross I cling.'

In worship and prayer Jesus Christ acts in our place and on our behalf in both a representative and a substitutionary way so that what he does in our stead is nevertheless effected as our very own, issuing freely and spontaneously out of ourselves. Through his incarnational and atoning union Jesus Christ has united himself with us in such a reconciling and sanctifying way that he interpenetrates and gathers up all our faltering, unclean worship and prayer into himself, assimilates them to his one self-oblation to God, so that when he presents himself as the worship and prayer of all creation, our worship and prayer are presented there also. When the Father accepts us in Jesus Christ his beloved Son, who then can distinguish our worship and prayer from Jesus' worship and prayer, for they are one and the same, wholly his and wholly ours in him?

Thus in all our worship and prayer, private and public, informal or formal, we come before God in such a way as to let Jesus Christ take our place, replacing our offering with his own self-offering, for he *is* the vicarious worship and prayer with which we respond to the love of the Father. We pray and worship in such a way as to make room in our prayer and worship for the living presence of Jesus as our Mediator in whom Offerer and Offering are one and the same, but in whom we are gathered up, with whom we are inseparably united, so that with him we pray and worship as we could not otherwise do.

At the end of the day when I kneel down and say my evening prayer, I know that no prayer of my own that I can offer to the heavenly Father is worthy of him or of power to avail with him, but all my prayer is made in the name of Jesus Christ alone as I rest in his vicarious prayer. It is then with utter peace and joy that I take into my mouth the Lord's Prayer which I am invited to pray through Jesus Christ, with him and in him, to God the Father, for in that prayer my poor, faltering, sinful prayer is not allowed to fall to the ground but is gathered up and presented to the Father in holy and eternally prevailing form. At the same time, I recall that the Father has promised to send the Spirit of his Son, mediated through the name and vicarious humanity of Jesus, into our hearts, crying, Abba, Father; and I am assured that as I pray in the name of God's beloved Son I am caught up with all my own infirmities within the inarticulate intercession of the eternal Spirit of the Father and of the Son from whose love nothing in heaven or earth, nothing in this world or in the world to come, can ever separate us.

(4) *The sacraments*

The holy sacraments, Baptism and Eucharist, are also acts of human response to the proclamation of the Gospel, dramatic answers to be given to the Word of God incarnate in Jesus Christ. That is certainly true, but they are above all divinely provided, dominically appointed ways of response and obedience of a radically vicarious kind. We recall that in the divinely instituted form and order of worship described in the Old Testament the people of Israel were not allowed to come before God with any kind of offering or sacrifice of their own choosing, or with some liturgy they had invented for themselves. From beginning to end all cultic acts were ordained by God and were to be regarded as the provision he had made for the way in which they were to respond to him in worship and prayer, supreme attention being given to the rites of circumcision and passover which had to do with the blood of the covenant upon which the whole structure and pattern of Israel's worship depended.

So it is here in the new covenant in which the divinely instituted forms of human response vicariously provided in Jesus Christ are represented by Baptism and Eucharist which

replace the rites of circumcision and passover in accordance
with the fundamental change in the covenant relation between God and his people brought about through the Incarnation and Atonement.

As such they are sacraments of the vicarious human
response to God effected by Jesus Christ in his representative
and substitutionary capacity in our place and on our behalf.
They are sacraments of the finished work of Christ to which
we can add nothing, sacraments which have as their substance and content none other than Jesus Christ clothed with
his Gospel of atoning mediation and reconciliation, and thus
sacraments which in their unique way represent the indivisible oneness of Christ's Word and Act and Person as Mediator between God and man. They are sacraments which by
their nature direct us away from ourselves to Jesus Christ in
whom all God's blessings for us are embodied, out of whose
fulness we receive grace for grace. Granted that they are
responses which we are commanded to make in our worship
of God, they are nevertheless not sacraments of what we do
but of what Christ Jesus has done in our place and on our
behalf. As such they are liturgical acts of prayer in the form
of divinely provided ordinances of response, sealing to us
within the new covenant our sharing in the vicarious obedience of Jesus Christ, the Servant-Son of God, offered once
and for all in his life and death in atoning exchange or
reconciliation of the world and through resurrection and
ascension presented to the Father in heavenly intercession
and advocacy for mankind.

There are two basic 'sacraments of the Gospel', one which
is given a form reflecting our once and for all union with
Christ and one which is given a form reflecting our continuous union and communion with him. Baptism is the sacrament of our incorporation into Christ on the ground of his
finished work, but while it is something which we are
commanded to do it is not a sacrament of what we do but of
what Christ has done for us, and corresponds more to the
substitutionary than the representative aspect of atonement.
It is the sacrament in which, so to speak, we are baptised out
of ourselves on the ground that Christ has taken our place. In

Baptism, therefore, we have expressed the character of faith in which our faith is implicated in the faith and faithfulness of Christ. Thus Baptism tells us that in our believing we do not rely upon our own faith but upon the vicarious faith of Christ which in sheer grace anticipates, generates, sustains and embraces the faith granted to those who are baptised. Hence St Paul reminded the Ephesians that it is by grace that we are saved through faith, and that is not our own doing for it is God's gift. Quite consistently we do not baptise ourselves but are baptised, for Baptism proclaims to us that we are saved by the unconditional grace of Christ alone, that we have been bought by the blood of Christ who has cleansed us and set the seal (*sphragis*) of his ownership upon us. As such Baptism constitutes the divinely provided witness (*martyria*) that we are no longer our own but belong to Jesus Christ our Redeemer and Lord. It is in that belonging that faith takes it source and out of it that it continues to grow.

The Lord's Supper or Eucharist, correspondingly, is the sacrament of our continuous participation in Jesus Christ and all he has done and continues to do for us by his grace, whereby we live unceasingly not from a centre in our selves or our own doing but from a centre in Christ and his doing. It is the sacrament of our union with the whole Jesus Christ, the incarnate, crucified, risen, ascended Son, both in respect of his ministry from the Father toward mankind and in respect of his ministry from mankind toward the Father. On the one hand, it is the sacrament of Christ's reconciling union with us in which he became bone of our bone and flesh of our flesh in order to take away our sin and guilt and pour out upon us the love of God; and as such it is the sacrament of the real presence of Christ in which we are given communion in his very body and blood and feed upon him as the bread of life. On the other hand, it is the sacrament of our union with him in his great act of self-consecration on our behalf that we might be consecrated through him, offering himself in holy obedience and atoning reconciliation to God on our behalf, that he might lift us up through his resurrection and ascension and present us in himself to the Father; and as such it is the sacrament in which we offer Christ eucharistically to the

Father through prayers and thanksgivings in Christ's name
as our only true worship, but in which the memorial of Christ
which we lift up before God is taken by Christ and
sanctifyingly assimilated into his own self-offering to the
Father through the eternal Spirit.

Thus the celebration of the Lord's Supper means that we
through the Spirit are so intimately united to Christ, by
communion in his body and blood, that we participate in his
self-consecration and self-offering to the Father made on our
behalf and in our place, and appear before the Majesty of God
in worship, praise and adoration with no other worship or
sacrifice than that which is identical with Christ Jesus our
Mediator and High Priest. We come to the Holy Table to
worship God, not protesting our own faith or conversion or
godliness, but proclaiming the death of Christ who through
his atoning exchange has replaced our poverty with his
boundless grace. And so we put out empty hands and bread
and wine are put into them which we eat and drink in
communion with his body and blood, for we have no other
offering with which to draw near to God but that one offering
which is identical with Jesus Christ himself, through whom,
with whom and in whom we glorify the Father.

(5) *Evangelism*

The Gospel is to be proclaimed in such a way that full place
is given to the man Jesus in his Person and Work as the
Mediator between God and man, otherwise it is not being
proclaimed in a way that corresponds with its actual message of unconditional grace and reconciling exchange. The
pattern had already been clearly set by our Lord when he
proclaimed that all who wished to be his disciples must
renounce themselves, or give up all right to themselves, take
up the cross and follow him, and when he laid it down as a
basic principle that those who want to save their lives will
lose them. Face to face with Christ all would-be followers
find themselves called into radical question, together with
their preconceptions, self-centred desires and self-will, for to
have him as Lord and Saviour means that he takes their place

in order to give them his place. The preaching of the Gospel in that radical form is not easy, for when we call upon people to repent and believe in Jesus Christ that they may be saved, we have great difficulty in doing that in such a way that we do not throw people back upon themselves in autonomous acts of personal repentance and decision, or encourage them to come to Christ for their own sake rather than for Christ's sake, in direct conflict with the very principle about motives laid down by Jesus.

There is, then, an evangelical way to preach the Gospel and an unevangelical way to preach it. The Gospel is preached in an unevangelical way, as happens so often in modern evangelism, when the preacher announces: This is what Jesus Christ has done for you, but you will not be saved *unless* you make your own personal decision for Christ as your Saviour. Or: Jesus Christ loved you and gave his life for you on the Cross, but you will be saved only *if* you give your heart to him. In that event what is actually coming across to people is not a Gospel of unconditional grace but some other Gospel of conditional grace which belies the essential nature and content of the Gospel as it is in Jesus. It was that subtle legalist twist to the Gospel which worried St Paul so much in his Epistle to the Galatians, a distortion of the truth which can easily take a 'gentile' as well as a 'Jewish' form. To preach the Gospel in that conditional or legalist way has the effect of telling poor sinners that in the last resort the responsibility for their salvation is taken off the shoulders of the Lamb of God and placed upon them — but in that case they feel that they will never be saved. They know perfectly well in their own hearts that if the chain that binds them to God in Jesus Christ has as even one of its links their own feeble act of decision, then the whole chain is as weak as that, its weakest link. They are aware that the very self who is being called upon to make such a momentous decision requires to be saved, so that the preaching of the Gospel would not really be good news unless it announced that in his unconditional love and grace Jesus Christ had put that human self, that ego of theirs, on an entirely different basis by being replaced at that crucial point by Jesus Christ himself.

How, then, is the Gospel to be preached in a genuinely evangelical way? Surely in such a way that full and central place is given to *the vicarious humanity of Jesus* as the all-sufficient human response to the saving love of God which he has freely and unconditionally provided for us. We preach and teach the Gospel evangelically, then, in such a way as this: God loves you so utterly and completely that he has given himself for you in Jesus Christ his beloved Son, and has thereby pledged his very Being as God for your salvation. In Jesus Christ God has actualised his unconditional love for you in your human nature in such a once for all way, that he cannot go back upon it without undoing the Incarnation and the Cross and thereby denying himself. Jesus Christ died for you precisely because you are sinful and utterly unworthy of him, and has thereby already made you his own before and apart from your ever believing in him. He has bound you to himself by his love in a way that he will never let you go, for even if you refuse him and damn yourself in hell his love will never cease. Therefore, repent and believe in Jesus Christ as your Lord and Saviour. From beginning to end what Jesus Christ has done for you he has done not only as God but as man. He has acted in your place in the whole range of your human life and activity, including your personal decisions, and your responses to God's love, and even your acts of faith. He has believed for you, fulfilled your human response to God, even made your personal decision for you, so that he acknowledges you before God as one who has already responded to God in him, who has already believed in God through him, and whose personal decision is already implicated in Christ's self-offering to the Father, in all of which he has been fully and completely accepted by the Father, so that in Jesus Christ you are already accepted by him. Therefore, renounce yourself, take up your cross and follow Jesus as your Lord and Saviour.

To preach the Gospel of the unconditional grace of God in that unconditional way is to set before people the astonishingly good news of what God has freely provided for us in the vicarious humanity of Jesus. To repent and believe in Jesus Christ and commit myself to him on that basis means that I do not need to look over my shoulder all the time to see whether I have really given myself personally to him, whether I really believe and trust him, whether my faith is at all adequate, for in faith it is not upon my faith, my believing or my personal commitment that I rely, but solely upon what Jesus Christ has done for me, in my place and on my behalf, and what he is and always will be as he stands in for me before the face of the Father. That means that I am completely liberated from all ulterior motives in believing or following Jesus Christ, for on the ground of his vicarious human response for me, I am free for spontaneous joyful response and worship and service as I could not otherwise be.

When Jesus Christ was born of the Virgin Mary, the underlying pattern governing all our human response to God was already established. To the announcement of the angel Mary responded with, 'Behold the handmaid of the Lord; be it unto me according to thy word.' She conceived and gave birth to Jesus, but that birth was not the result of a synergistic activity on the part of Mary and God, for it came about as the result of a creative act of the Holy Spirit and as the manifestation of the unconditional grace of God. Mary was not treated like an impersonal instrument in the hands of God but graciously blessed, sanctified and upheld in the freedom and integrity of her human being within the reciprocal relationship with God to which she belonged in Israel. And Jesus, born among us as a human being by the grace of God alone, was far from being a puppet in the hands of God, but on the contrary the only human being who has ever lived with perfect freedom and perfect humanity, and as such became, as we have seen, the humanising Man and the personalising Person who is the creative source of all human and personal relations with God. It is as such that Jesus Christ meets us in the Gospel, exhibiting in his own human life and being what happens to us in and through him by the grace of God alone. Jesus Christ in his humanity stands for the fact that 'all of grace' does not mean 'nothing of man', but the very reverse, the restoration of full and authentic human being in the spontaneity and freedom of human response to the love of God. Thus the Virgin Birth of Jesus may be taken as the paradigm of the way that the saving grace of God takes with us when we are called to repent and believe in Jesus Christ and his Gospel.

Let all this be granted, as surely we must in fidelity to the nature of the Gospel. However, there is still the practical problem we have to reckon with in evangelism: how to proclaim Christ and his Gospel calling for a response in 'the obedience of faith' in such a way that we do not thereby provoke and indirectly support the self-centred human ego in its claim to an 'inviolable right' over its own decisions, or even reinforce the self-will of that ego in its response to God. To that practical problem in evangelism, Christ has provided us with a practical answer in the sacraments of the Gospel which proclaim in act what we find it difficult to make clear by word alone.

The sacrament of Baptism, administered to those who repent and believe in Jesus Christ and to their children, proclaims to them that they are saved by Christ alone and not even in a subsidiary way through their own repenting and believing. In Baptism they are baptised out of a centre in their own repenting and believing into a centre in Christ who died for them and rose again, so that Baptism seals to them the fact that their old selves with all their vaunted 'rights' have been crucified and renounced in Christ, and that they have been given new being through his resurrection in which they are freed from the shackles of the past. Baptism proclaims to them the good news that Christ has made them his own, and that they belong to him, and that it is on that ground and from that source that the whole life of faith in Christ and obedience to him develops. Thus with Baptism the Gospel is proclaimed by act and not in word only in a way that really corresponds to the actual content of the Gospel.

In the sacrament of the Lord's Supper there also takes place a proclamation of the Gospel, for as often as we break the bread and drink from the cup we proclaim the Lord's death till he come. There it is announced to us that the word of forgiveness of sins proclaimed by Jesus Christ was not forgiveness in word only but in power, for it was enacted in his sacrifice for sin on the Cross and wholly made good in his

resurrection from the dead, so that instead of our sins separating us from God they are made to serve the reconciling
love of God which binds us inseparably to him in Jesus
Christ. Thus in Holy Communion the Gospel of Christ is
communicated to us in an enacted form, for as surely as we
eat the bread and drink the wine and they become part of our
flesh and blood existence, so surely we are made by grace to
partake of Jesus Christ himself in his body and blood in a way
that no mere words can convey. Moreover, in this Holy
Supper Christ has provided us with a way of feeding upon
him as the life-giving bread so that we may live continually
out of our true centre in him and not out of a centre in
ourselves. Hence throughout the whole of our Christian life
and service we are brought to rely not on any obedience or
righteousness of our own but upon the grace of God incarnate in Jesus Christ, who for our sakes became poor that we
through his poverty might become rich.

Quite clearly the word and sacraments belong together.
The Gospel as it is proclaimed in and by the sacraments
belongs to evangelism as much as the Gospel proclaimed in
word. Christ communicates himself to us through both and
through both together, providing us in different ways with
the appropriate human response which we cannot make
ourselves but through which the Gospel becomes established in us. In virtue of the sacraments the proclamation of
Christ is not fruitless but accomplishes its purpose, and then
the sacraments themselves fulfil their appointed end as
sacraments of the Word who became flesh and who alone
speaks to us words that are life and spirit. Thus, to use earlier
terminology, the sacraments of Baptism and Holy Communion are not to be regarded merely as 'confirming ordinances'
but as 'converting ordinances', for in and through them the
Gospel strikes home to us in such a way as to draw us within
the vicarious response to God which Jesus Christ constitutes
in his own humanity, the humanity which he took from us
and converted back to God the Father in himself. It is not
surprising, therefore, that it is in the actual celebration of the
sacraments, not only of Holy Baptism but of Holy Communion, that 'the word of the truth of the Gospel' is received and

grasped as it could not otherwise be, in Jesus Christ himself.

In conclusion, let me direct you to those striking words of St Paul in his Epistle to the Galatians, 2:20, which give succinct expression to the evangelical truth which we have been trying to clarify. 'I am crucified with Christ: nevertheless I live, yet not I but Christ lives in me; and the life which I now live in the flesh I live by faith, the *faithfulness* of the Son of God who loved me and gave himself for me.' This is surely the insight that we must allow to inform all our human responses to God, whether they be in faith, conversion and personal decision, worship and prayer, the holy sacraments, or the proclamation of the Gospel: '*I yet not I but Christ*'. This applies even to faith. I am convinced that the peculiar expression which St Paul used to express the faith-relationship with Christ should be translated as I have rendered it, but even if it is translated as 'by faith in the Son of God', the self-correction made by St Paul applies, 'not I but Christ'. That is to say, when I say 'I believe' or 'I have faith', I must correct myself and add 'not I but Christ in me'. That is the message of the vicarious humanity of Jesus Christ on which the Gospel tells me I may rely: that Jesus Christ in me believes in my place and at the same time takes up my poor faltering and stumbling faith into his — 'Lord, I believe,help my unbelief' — embracing, upholding and undergirding it through his invariant faithfulness. That is the kind of faith which will never fail. But this applies to the whole of my life in Christ and to all my human responses to God, for in Jesus Christ they are laid hold of, sanctified and informed by his vicarious life of obedience and response to the Father. They are in fact so indissolubly united to the life of Jesus Christ which he lived out among us and which he has offered to the Father, as arising out of our human being and nature, that they are *our responses* toward the love of the Father poured out upon us through the mediation of the Son and in the unity of his Holy Spirit.

CHAPTER 5

The Atonement and the Holy Trinity

In earlier chapters attention has been focused upon the
difficulties that arise in various fields of knowledge when
elements of reality that are naturally integrated have been
torn apart from each other through the prevalence of dualist
and analytical modes of thought. We discussed the damaging effect of these ways of thinking in the mediation of
revelation and of reconciliation, not least in view of the
disrupted relation between the Christian Church and Israel
the covenanted people of God and the historic bearer of
divine revelation to mankind. But we also faced the problem
that can arise at the very centre of the Christian Faith in our
understanding of the Person of Jesus Christ, the one Mediator between God and man, who is himself both God and man.
In this chapter discussion is carried back into the ultimate
doctrine of God, not only as he is toward us in Christ but as
he is eternally in himself. We probe into the effect of dualist
ways of thinking upon knowledge of God, and consider the
deeper understanding of him made possible by the cross of
Christ as through him both Jews and gentiles have access by
one Spirit to the Father.

A dualist approach to knowledge of God is particularly
characteristic of Western theology, whether in the Roman
Catholic or in the Protestant tradition. This is very evident in
Roman text-book theology developed under the impact of St
Thomas Aquinas which carries within it what Karl Barth
called a 'split concept of God', for it operates first with a basic

idea of the one essence of God, and only subsequently offers
an account of the three Persons in God, without any intrinsic
relation between them. Thus a clear distinction was drawn
between the doctrine of *The One God* and the doctrine of *The
Triune God*, upheld in our day by Bernard Lonergan, but
rejected, under the influence of Barth and Greek Orthodox
theology, by Karl Rahner. The effect of this dualist approach,
as Rahner has argued, is to isolate the doctrine of the Holy
Trinity within the general body of dogmatic theology and to
give it no integral place in the world and in salvation history.
Moreover, as Karl Barth had argued, this approach detaches
the triune understanding of God from the essential content of
God's self-revelation. That is to say, the doctrine of the
Trinity becomes attached to an independently reached doctrine of the one God, and is not regarded, therefore, as
essentially and inseparably integrated with it.

It is not very different with classical Protestant formulations, as one can see, for example, in the Westminster Confession of Faith. Thus in chapter two, 'Of God, and of the Holy
Trinity', the main paragraphs are devoted to an account of
the infinite being of God and his attributes expressed in
rather abstract and negative terms, to which two brief sen-
tences are appended on the Trinity. As is made clear in the
Larger and Shorter Catechisms, the doctrine of God set out in
this Westminster theology is by way of answer to an impersonal question about *what* the essence of God is thought to be,
and not by way of answer to the personal question as to *who*
God is as he has actually made himself personally known to
us through Jesus Christ and in the Holy Spirit. What is
offered is a doctrine of God behind the back of his self-
revelation, without any direct relation to his saving acts in
history or his gracious condescension to be one with us and
to give himself freely for us in reconciling sacrifice. Because
this doctrine of the Trinity is only added on to an independently conceived doctrine of the one God, without being
internally integrated with it, it is hardly surprising that it has
little actual bearing throughout the Confession of Faith or the
Catechisms upon the nature and content of the Gospel or
upon Christian devotion and life. In point of fact the doctrine

of God offered there is not essentially or distinctively Christian, for it is not a doctrine of God as the Father of our Lord Jesus Christ in whom and in the Holy Spirit we have to do directly and immediately with God himself.

Christian and Jewish Conceptions of God

Of course the question must be asked how the Christian conception of God as Father, Son and Holy Spirit squares with the understanding of the Lord God Almighty, the *I am who I am*, or *I shall be who I shall be*, revealed to Israel throughout its history, and through Israel and the Old Testament Scriptures to all mankind, as the one God of heaven and earth apart from whom there is no other God. That is a question that was already posed and met in the New Testament Scriptures, in which no other God is acknowledged than the one God of the Old Testament Scriptures. Thus Jesus himself took on his own lips the essential confession of the Jewish tradition: 'Hear, O Israel, the Lord our God, the Lord is one.' It was in no contradiction to this when Christians acknowledged that 'Jesus is Lord', for they believed that in him *Immanuel* had come, 'God with us', in an incarnate way. Thus central to the Christian message was the supreme truth of the Deity of the Lord Jesus Christ in perfect oneness with the Deity of God the Father. In Christ the covenanted purpose of God embodied in the people of Israel throughout long ages has been brought to its climax in such a way that in him as the Son and Word of God become flesh, the self-revealing of the one God has completed its own movement in the reconciliation of mankind to God. As we have already seen in the second chapter, the mediation of revelation and the mediation of reconciliation are intertwined with one another.

All authentic knowledge involves a cognitive union of the mind with its object, which calls for the removal of any estrangement or alienation that may obstruct or distort it. This applies not less but in fact supremely to our knowledge of God. That is why God's unique self-revelation to the

people of Israel plunged it into such a prolonged ordeal of
tension between it and Yahweh, and why the covenanted
relations between God and Israel could not be maintained
without unceasing attention to God's provision for reconciliation through atoning sacrifice. God's revelation of himself
to mankind through Israel could not take root and come to
expression in human being and knowing apart from the
ever-deepening enactment of the holy Word and Truth of
God in the very existence of Israel, and therefore without the
painful transforming and reconciling of its fundamental cast
of mind. But this unique relation of Israel to God has had the
effect of making the Jews appear a singularly strange and
odd people among the nations of the world, alienating it
from them, and thereby intensifying its pain. The closer the
bonds of God's covenant love with Israel were drawn, the
more Israel was inwardly shaped and moulded by the presence of God to be the unique bearer of divine revelation and
the chosen instrument of his saving purpose of salvation for
all the peoples of the world. Thus the whole course of God's
historical interaction with Israel as presented to us in the Old
Testament Scriptures made clear that revelation and reconciliation must be locked into each other, for neither can reach
its destined end without the other.

As we have already noted in our discussion of the mediation of reconciliation, the fulfilment of God's revealing and
saving purpose in Jesus Christ did not mean that the ancient
covenant of God with Israel was abolished, but rather that it
retained its force in the divine election of Israel as the people
to whom were committed the oracles of God. They constituted the appointed ground upon which and from which the
mission and expansion of divine salvation to all mankind
broke forth from Israel into the world and became established among the gentile nations. Thus the one covenant of
grace forged by God with Israel entered a new dispensation
in the foundation of the Christian Church as the missionary
community entrusted with the message of the Gospel, without abrogation of the promises of God made to Israel set forth
in the Old Testament Scriptures. Henceforth the roles and
destinies of Israel and the Church were locked into each

other. With the accomplishment of reconciliation in Jesus Christ in the midst of Israel, reconciliation was no longer just a promise announced through divine revelation to Israel, but the actualisation of that promise in the advent of Immanuel, God with us and God for us. That is to say, reconciliation constitutes the inner dynamic content of revelation, and revelation becomes effective precisely as reconciliation for thereby it achieves its end. Hence Jews and Christians need and complement each other both in their service of divine revelation and in their service of divine reconciliation, and cannot but frustrate their dual mission from God to mankind when they are estranged from one another.

The interdependence of the mission of Israel and the mission of the Christian Church was one of the primary questions to which St Paul addressed himself, for it was of acute significance in his own case. As an Israelite, a Hebrew of the Hebrews, he insisted that the gift and calling of God to the Jews were irrevocable, while as the Apostle to the Gentiles he was unashamedly committed to the Gospel of Christ as the power of God unto salvation to every one who believes, to the Jew first and also to the Greek. Let us turn particularly to the second chapter of the Epistle to the Ephesians (11-22), written I believe by St Paul himself, which has to do with this interlocking of the mission of Jews and Christians, of prophets and apostles, and as such has a direct bearing upon the subject of this chapter 'the Atonement and the Holy Trinity'.

In what St Paul says there he clearly has in mind the fact that the whole of the raised area on which the Temple stood in Jerusalem was surrounded by a barrier within which no gentile was allowed to pass – St Paul refers to it as 'the middle wall of partition'. It was designed to separate the holy from the unholy, those who were allowed to draw near to God in worship from those who were 'far off' or beyond the pale, strangers to the covenants of promise. We may well think here of the parable that Jesus told of the man who made a great supper to which he invited many people. When they refused to come, he sent his servants out into the streets and lanes of the city to bring in the poor, the maimed, the blind and lame, and even to summon those who were beyond the barriers, that is, the excommunicated and the unclean who were prevented by rules and regulations of the Jewish law from drawing near to God, for the feast was now thrown open to them.

And let us also remember what took place on the Day of Pentecost, when the Holy Spirit was poured out with power upon the disciples and their followers. In explanation of what was happening St Peter pointed to the words of the prophet Joel that in the last days God would pour out his Spirit upon all flesh, when whoever called upon the name of the Lord would be saved. That great day had now come, he claimed, for the very Jesus whom the rulers had put to death on the cross had been raised by God from the dead and had received from the Father the promised Holy Spirit who was now poured out upon his people. In proclaiming to the Jews who thronged the Temple area that the man Jesus whom they had crucified was both their Lord and Messiah, Peter called upon them to repent and be baptised in the name of Christ for the remission of sins and they would receive the gift of the Holy Spirit. Then he added 'for the promise is to you and your children, and to all that are afar off, even as many as the Lord our God shall call'. In other words, it was not only Jews and their children within the barriers that might draw near to God and receive the Spirit but those beyond the barriers as well. Access to God was now open to all through the cross of Christ and the actual presence of his Holy Spirit.

St Paul had the same point in mind when he wrote to the Christians of Ephesus as follows. 'Remember that as uncircumcised gentiles you were once without Christ and were excluded from the community of Israel, strangers to the covenants and their promises, without hope and even without God in the world, but now in Christ Jesus you who used to be far off have been brought near by the blood of Christ. For he is our peace who has made us both one, and has broken down the middle wall of partition between us, thereby bringing hostility to an end in his own flesh, for he made the rules and regulations of the law ineffective, so that he might create in himself a single new humanity, thus making peace.

By his cross Christ has reconciled both Jews and gentiles in one body to God, putting an end in himself to all enmity between them. And so Christ came and proclaimed the Gospel of peace, to you who were far off and to you who were near, for through him we both have access in one Spirit to the Father. Hence you gentiles are no longer strangers and exiles but fellow-citizens with the holy people and members of the family of God. You are built upon the foundation of the apostles and the prophets, with Jesus Christ himself as its cornerstone. In him the whole building is joined together and becomes a holy temple in the Lord, and in him you are built together into a home where God dwells through his Spirit.'

What does this have to tell us about the interlocking of the mission of Israel and the mission of the Christian Church in respect of both revelation and reconciliation, and in respect of the doctrine of the one God advocated by Judaism and the doctrine of the Triune God advocated by Christianity? Two points in particular need to be considered: the fact that the Christian understanding of God is grounded in and inseparable from the revelation of the one Lord God Almighty given to Israel and mediated to us in the Old Testament Scriptures; and the fact that there is no access to knowledge of God as he is in himself apart from the reconciliation with God brought about by the cross of Christ. In their understanding of God Christians and Jews need to be reconciled to God and to each other.

Christian and Jewish Approaches to God Need Each Other

St Paul insists that it is only as gentiles are incorporated into the covenant people of God and thus made members of God's household, or, as he says elsewhere, are grafted like wild olive branches on to the trunk of Israel, that they may share with them in the revelation of the one true God uniquely mediated to them. They must remember that the branches do not bear the trunk, but the trunk bears the branches. Separated from Israel gentiles have to do only with some unrevealed God who is not God, and are in fact 'without hope and without God (*atheoi*) in the world'. As our Lord himself said to the woman of Samaria, 'You worship what you do not know, we worship what we know, for salvation is of the Jews'. It was much the same thing that St Paul said to the Athenians on Mars hill when he proclaimed to them the one whom they ignorantly worshipped. The point that St Paul makes here is that the knowledge Christians have of God is rooted and grounded in the real knowledge of God which the Jews have for it was to them that God committed the sacred oracles. We must not forget that the Holy Scriptures which Jesus himself acknowledged and used were the Hebrew Scriptures of the people of Israel. The God and Father of our Lord Jesus Christ was none other than the God of Abraham, Isaac and Jacob, the one God of Moses and the prophets. Christian knowledge of God is founded, then, St Paul tells us, not only upon the apostles but upon the prophets.

We have already had occasion in the first Chapter to discuss the inextricable interrelation between God's self-revelation in Jesus and his self-revelation through Israel, when we examined the fundamental importance for our understanding of Jesus himself of Jewish ways of thought moulded by God throughout the long historical ordeal to which he deliberately subjected them through his Word. Once we allow Jesus to be abstracted from his setting in the context of Israel and its vicarious mission in divine revelation, our gentile approach to him as Christ, whether in the West and or in the East, seriously damages our understanding of him and distorts the image of Christ which the Church presents to the world. This applies not least to our relations with our Jewish brethren who cannot recognise in 'our Christ' their promised 'Messiah' who according to Daniel would be cut off, but not for himself. At this point our particular concern is with the fact that Christian understanding of God as Trinity must not be, and cannot really be, divorced from Jewish understanding of God as One, otherwise it also becomes distorted through alien patterns of thought which our gentile minds and cultures impose upon it. The doctrine of the Trinity is not a doctrine of three Gods, but a doctrine of the one Lord God with a profounder understanding of the inner unity of his eternal being. What, then, about the bearing of Christian trinitarian understanding of God upon Jewish unitarian understanding of him?

What is at stake here is the tendency we have already noted in Western theology to allow analytical and dualist ways of thinking to separate the doctrine of the One God from the doctrine of the Triune God, as though the doctrine of the three divine Persons were not intrinsically and essentially integrated with the doctrine of the one indivisible being of God. Apart from that integration trinitarianism constantly threatens to pass over into some form of tritheism. And so what is also at stake here is the seriousness with which we understand divine reconciliation as the inner dynamic of God's unitary self-revelation, and thus the question of whether we are given through reconciliation with God access in some measure to what he is in his inner life as the one ever-living God, who made himself ineffably known to Moses and the people of Israel as *Jahweh, I am who I am* or *I shall be who I shall be.* This is the crucial issue to which we must attend in Paul's argument in the passage cited from his Epistle to the Ephesians: the inner relation between the doctrine of atonement and the doctrine of the triune God.

As St Paul learned in his own experience, access to knowledge of God as he is in himself is not given to us apart from God's self-revelation through the medium of Israel, on the one hand, or apart from reconciliation with God through the cross of Christ, on the other hand. Jesus Christ himself is not to be understood as Mediator between God and man except through the interpretative framework prepared by God through his covenant relations with Israel for the advent of the Saviour into the world. Nor is our mediation with God to be realised apart from the reconciling blood of Christ by which he broke down the dividing barriers between gentile and Jew and indeed between both of them and God. That is to say, it is only on the basis of reconciliation to God that through Christ we both, Jews and gentiles, have access by one Spirit to the Father. Apart from the mediation of Christ the people of Israel can know God only in his undifferentiated oneness and not as he is in his intrinsic trinitarian relations.

And apart from the instructive patterns of thought which God has forged in human understanding and provided for all mankind through the medium of Israel, Jesus Christ and his death on the Cross are a bewildering enigma. Moreover, apart from the atonement the Holy Spirit, the immediate presence of God himself to his people, would not have been poured out at Pentecost, and we would be unable to draw near to God and enter into personal communion with him, for as sinful human beings we could not endure his holiness.

The transcendent holiness and unapproachable majesty of God had been indelibly imprinted upon the memory and soul of Israel, not only through the awesome law-giving at Mount Sinai, but through the sacred liturgy prescribed by the Word of God for the annual celebration of the Day of Atonement in the Tabernacle or the Temple, when God's covenant with Israel was renewed. It was at the risk of his life and only under cover of the blood of atoning sacrifice that the High Priest representing all Israel could enter through the veil into the immediate presence of God in the Holy of Holies, and bring back to the people of Israel the peace of God in renewal of his covenant mercies. The sacrifices and oblations offered by the High Priest were not regarded as having any efficacy in themselves, but as having efficacy only in so far as they were acts of liturgical obedience bearing witness to the fact that it is only God himself who can make atonement for sin and effect reconciliation. As such *Yom Kippur* or Day of Atonement in the liturgical year carried within it the promise of a final Day of Atonement when God himself would provide the Lamb for sacrifice and cleanse his people from their sin, making them holy as he himself is holy.

That is, we believe, precisely what was fulfilled in Jesus Christ and his death upon the cross, and fulfilled once for all, not in liturgical repetition, but in the flesh of Christ Jesus who, as both the atoning sacrifice and our High Priest, entered through the veil into the immediate presence of the Most High. Three evangelists tell us significantly that at crucifixion of Jesus the veil of the Temple in Jerusalem was actually rent down the middle. By his blood Christ has reconciled us to God and thereby opened the way for all who

believe in his name to enter with him into the holy presence
of God and share in the gift of the Holy Spirit which he
received from the Father. Thus through the grace of the Lord
Jesus Christ and the Communion of the Holy Spirit we sinful
human beings may have access to the love of Father, and
know him not from afar but intimately as he is in himself. It
is through faith in Jesus Christ that we are justified and have
peace with God - otherwise we remain in our sins, unforgiven,
and alienated from his grace, with only the fearful prospect
of divine judgment before us.

Necessity of the Atonement for Knowledge of the Trinity

Let us draw out the implications of St Paul's teaching a little
further. Divine revelation and reconciliation, as we have
seen, involve a two-way movement between God and man,
so that in reaching an understanding of God as triune we
have to take into account not only our drawing near to God
but God's drawing near to us in and through the self-
humiliation of his Son in the incarnation and crucifixion, for
it is thus that God in boundless love and unlimited grace has
lowered himself to be one with us, really given himself to us,
and made himself knowable by us within the lowly conditions of our creaturely and alienated existence. The fact that
Jesus Christ is God's beloved Son means that in him the
Father was actively and personally present in the crucifixion
of Christ, intervening redemptively in our lostness and
darkness. In giving his beloved Son in atoning sacrifice for
our sin God has given himself to us in unreserved love, so
that the cross is not only a revelation of the love of Christ but
a revelation of the love of God. The cross was a window into
the very heart of God, for in and behind the cross, it was God
the Father himself who paid the cost of our salvation. And so
through the shedding of the blood of Christ in atoning
sacrifice for our sin the innermost nature of God the Father as
holy compassionate love has been revealed to us.

This teaching is also relevant to our understanding of the
nature of the Holy Spirit who as the Spirit of the Father and
of the Son intervenes in vicarious intercession on our behalf

and pours out the love of God into our hearts. Pentecost and Calvary belong inseparably and integrally together, for the outpouring of the Holy Spirit upon us belongs to the fulfilment of God's reconciling of the world to himself. This connection between the cross of Christ and the mission of Spirit is clearly indicated in the interpretative aside offered by St John to our Lord's promise of living water to those who believe on him: 'This he said about the Spirit, whom those who believed in him were to receive, for as yet the Spirit had not been given, because Jesus was not yet glorified.'

It is not too much to say, then, that *the proper understanding of God as Father, Son and Holy Spirit takes place only within the movement of atoning propitiation whereby God draws near to us and draws us near to himself in believing response and brings us into union with himself through the gift of his Spirit,* for it is only within that two-way movement of reconciling love that God's self-revelation to mankind attains its end. Through Christ and his awful self-sacrifice on the cross alone may we sinful and alienated human beings have access by one Spirit to the Father. By 'propitiation', of course, is not meant any placating or conciliating of God on our part, for God is never acted upon by means of priestly sacrifice offered by human beings. Thus as in the Old Testament liturgy it is always God himself who provides the sacrifice whereby he draws near to the worshipper and draws the worshipper near to himself, so in the actualised liturgy of the life, death, resurrection and ascension of Jesus Christ, it is God himself who in atoning propitiation draws near to us and draws us near to himself. God does not love us, Calvin once wrote, because he has reconciled us to himself; it is because he loved us that he has reconciled us to himself.

Propitiation is wholly from beginning to end the movement of God's forgiving and expiating love whereby in the initiative and freedom of his own divine being he acts both from the side of God as God toward man and from the side of man as man toward God. Thereby in the form of a relation of himself to himself, God bridges in his incarnate life in the Lord Jesus Christ the fearful chasm of alienation between man and himself, uniting himself with us under his own righteous judgment upon sin in order to bear and expiate our guilt, all in himself as the one Mediator between God and man who is himself very God and very man. That is the astonishing event which St Paul once described as the justification of the ungodly! It is precisely in this propitiating movement of reconciliation and justification through his Son that God the Father opens his innermost heart and mind to us in the self-revelation of his love, and through the communion of his Spirit makes himself present to us within the conditions of our creaturely existence in such a healing and creative way as to open our hearts and minds to receive and understand his self-revelation as Father, Son and Holy Spirit. At the same time we are brought to know that what he is toward us in this propitiating movement as Father, Son and Holy Spirit, he is in himself, in the immanent relations of his one eternal and transcendent being as God the Father Almighty, Creator of heaven and earth and of all things visible and invisible.

The key to this ontological connection between what is called 'the economic Trinity' and 'the immanent Trinity' was carefully expressed at the Council of Nicaea in 315 AD as the *homoousion*, the oneness in being, or sameness in being, between the incarnate Son and God the Father, a term which the great theologians of the Early Church soon applied rightly to the relation of the Holy Spirit to the Godhead as well. It gave expression to the teaching of the New Testament that there is an unbroken relation in being and act between the incarnate Son and God the Father, and likewise between the Holy Spirit and God the Father. Jesus Christ and the Holy Spirit are to be acknowledged as God in the same sense as the Father is acknowledged as God. This supreme truth has already come before us in the chapter on 'The Person of the Mediator'.

If the Lord Jesus Christ is, as the Nicene Creed expressed it, the only-begotten Son of the Father, begotten from his Father before all ages, true God of true God, then the Father/Son or Son/Father relation falls within the eternal being of God, the Sonship of Christ being just as eternal in God as the Fatherhood of God, for God the Father is not Father apart from the Son, and God the Son is not Son apart from the Father. The revelation of God in the saving acts of Jesus Christ as Father and Son is grounded in and issues from the inner being of the one eternal God. Hence when Jesus Christ reveals God the Father to us in and through himself as the only-begotten Son, he gives us access to knowledge of God as he really is in his divine nature: what God is toward us in the revealing and saving acts of Jesus Christ he is in eternally and immanently in himself, and what God is in himself eternally and immanently as Father and Son he actually is toward us in the revealing and saving acts of Jesus Christ. The same movement of belief and thought applies completely to the Holy Spirit as well, to his relation in being to the Father and the Son. Hence we believe that the trinitarian relations of God as Father, Son and Holy Spirit made known to us in the Gospel, derive from and direct us back to ultimate trinitarian relations in the eternal being of the one and only God.

We must now give fuller attention to two considerations: the ground of atoning propitiation in the trinitarian relations in God, and the participation given to us through the Holy Spirit in God's knowledge of himself.

The Trinitarian Ground of Atonement

(1) Since Jesus Christ the only-begotten Son of God is of one being with the Father, and since he is God and man inseparably united in his incarnate Person, then like the incarnation the atoning work of the incarnate Son falls within the inner life of the Holy Trinity. It certainly took place in the historical life and activity of the Lord Jesus Christ from his birth to his resurrection, and supremely in his death on the cross, but it also took place in God. As we have already noted, the cross is not only a revelation of the love of Christ but a revelation of the love of God. The cross is a window opened into the very heart of God. The fact that the Father did not spare his only Son but delivered him up for us all, as St Paul expressed it, tells us that in the sacrifice of Christ on the cross it was the Father as well as the Son who paid the cost of our

salvation, so that through the blood of Christ the innermost nature of God the Father as holy love became revealed to us. However, we must also say that as the incarnate Son is of one and the same being as God the Father, so the atoning act perfected in the cross of Jesus Christ is grounded in the very being of the eternal God, that is, in the eternal being of the Holy Trinity.

As Athanasius and Karl Barth in their different ways have shown us, God's activity is not separate from his being but inheres in his being: it is his being-in-act or his act-in-being, not something in addition to his being but his very being in action. Thus the atonement is to be regarded as the act of God in his being and his being in his act. This is not to say, of course, that it was the Father who was crucified, for it was the Son in his distinction from the Father who died on the cross, but it is to say that the suffering of Christ on the cross was not just human, it was divine as well as human, and in fact is to be regarded as the suffering of God himself, that is, as the being of God in his redeeming act, and the passion of God in his very being as God. Likewise, as we shall discuss later, this applies also the act and being of God the Holy Spirit, although it was the Son and not the Holy Spirit who died on the cross. Thus we cannot but think of the atonement as a threefold act grounded in and issuing from the triune being of God. While the Father, the Son and the Holy Spirit are personally distinct from one another, they are nevertheless of one and the same being with one another in God, and their acts interpenetrate one another in the indivisibility of the one Godhead.

In the symbolism of the Old Testament liturgy the act of atonement was brought to its completion in the Holy of Holies as the sacrificial blood was sprinkled upon the mercy seat of God. Thus the atonement was regarded as an ineffable mystery that takes place in the innermost sanctum completely hidden from public gaze. Likewise, according to the Epistle to the Hebrews, we must think of the atoning act of Christ our great High Priest who through the eternal Spirit offered himself without blemish to the Father, penetrating through the veil of all created realities into the innermost sanctum of God's holy presence. No explanation is ever given in the New Testament, or in the Old Testament, why atonement for sin involves the blood of sacrifice. Just as God's love, so God's atoning act, knows no 'Why?'. The ultimate reason of God's act of atonement, like the ultimate reason of his love, is none other than God himself. The atonement is not to be explained or understood simply on the ground of the historical event of the crucifixion of Jesus, as some external transaction enacted by Jesus between God and man describable in moral or legal terms, but as taking place ultimately within the incarnate mystery of the union of divine and human nature in Jesus Christ the Mediator between God and man, and thus as ineffable inexplicable mystery hidden in God himself. There is no conflict between the act and being of Christ and the act and being of God, for there is an unbroken relation of being and act between them, which applies fully to their act and being in the atonement. The atoning self-sacrifice of Christ that took place once for all on the cross was offered through the eternal Spirit to God thus procuring eternal redemption. As such the atonement as well as being an historical event is not a transitory but a final event, an eternally enduring operation, even though it was not something that had ever happened before. Just as the creation was a new event, new even for God, for while God was always Father, he was not always Creator; and just as the incarnation was a new event, new even for God, for the Son of God was not always incarnate; so the atonement was a new act, new even for God. Nevertheless as the act of Christ through the eternal Spirit, as the act of God in his ever-living being, it is God's very own act eternally grounded in himself and hidden in the ultimate mystery of his triune being.

It should now be clear that the oneness of God's being and act in the incarnation and the atonement once for all bridges the relation between man and God, history and eternity. Jesus Christ himself, God and man in his one Person, is the way, the truth and the life, and there is no other way to the Father. In him priest and sacrifice, offering and the offerer are one, so that he constitutes in himself the new and living way opened up for us into God's immediate presence. He is our

Forerunner, our High Priest, in whom our hope is lodged as
an anchor sure and steadfast that reaches beyond the veil of
sense and time into the heavenly world. In him God has
drawn near to us, and we may draw near to God with
complete confidence as those who are sanctified together
with Jesus, and who are included in his atoning self-presentation through the eternal Spirit to the Father. That is surely
what it means for us sinners to have access to the Father
through the blood of Christ and in one Spirit, and on that
ground of divine propitiation and reconciliation which God
himself has freely provided for us to be allowed really to
draw near to God in the personal response of faith and to
know him as he is in himself, and, what is more, to be certain
that what he is toward us in the Gospel of Christ as Father,
Son and Holy Spirit, he really is and always will be in himself.
It is thus through the union of God and man and the atonement embodied in the incarnate Person of the Lord Jesus
Christ that we have the all-important connection in being
and act between 'the economic Trinity' and 'the immanent
Trinity'.

The Communion of the Spirit

(2) Since only God can really know God, we may know him
only as he reveals *himself* to us *through* himself. That is what
takes place when through the communion of the Holy Spirit
we are enabled by grace to share in God's knowledge of
himself. It will help our understanding of this if we bring
together two biblical passages, one from the Gospels, St
Matthew 11.25-27 (or St Luke 10.21-22), and one from St
Paul's First Epistle to the Corinthians, 2.9-12. In the first
passage our Lord is recorded as saying: "I thank you Father,
Lord of heaven and earth, that you have hidden these things
from the wise and understanding and revealed them to
children. Yes, Father, for this was your gracious will. All
things have been delivered to me by my Father; and no one
knows the Son except the Father, and no one knows the
Father except the Son and anyone to whom the Son chooses
to reveal him." In the second passage St Paul wrote: "'What

no eye has seen, nor ear heard, nor the heart of man conceived, what God has prepared for those who love him', God has revealed to us through the Spirit. For the Spirit searches everything, even the depths of God. For who is there among men who knows the depths of a man except his own spirit within him? So also no one knows the depths of God except the Spirit of God. Now we have received not the spirit of the world, but the Spirit who is from God, that we might know the things graciously given to us by God."

In the first of these citations we learn that there is a closed circle of knowing between the Father and the Son and the Son and the Father. The Father and the Son are inherently and reciprocally related with one another in God in such an exclusive way that there is no knowledge of the Son except that of the Father, and no knowledge of the Father except that of the Son. And so there is no way for us to know the Son except through the Father, and no way for us to know the Father except through the Son, unless a way is freely opened up by the Son for us to share in the communion of knowing within God himself. That is precisely what may happen through the revealing activity of Jesus Christ the incarnate Son and Word of God, for in him God has anchored within our human existence the mutual knowing which the Father and the Son have of one another, so that it is in union with him and through him that we human beings may share in the knowledge which the Father and the Son have with one another.

In the second citation we learn how this knowing of God through God actually takes place - through receiving the Spirit of God who is sent to us from God. By dwelling in God the Spirit knows what God is within the immanent depths of his divine being, and by dwelling in us he reveals to us hidden depths in God which could not otherwise be known or conceived by any human being. Thus it is through the communion of the Holy Spirit who is God and dwells in God, that we may share in the inner communion between the Father and the Son, and participate in their knowing of one another. The Holy Spirit is the Spirit of the Father and the Son, who in being given to us enables us beyond any capacity of our own to participate in God's knowing of himself through himself, and thus really to know the one God in the inner relations of his divine being, as Father, Son and Holy Spirit. To express it the other way round, through Christ Jesus, through his cross and in union with him, we are given access to the Father in one Spirit, and know him to be eternally in himself the Father, the Son and the Holy Spirit which he is toward us in his revealing and saving activity.

We must bear in mind here not only the coinherent and reciprocal relations between the Father and the Son, but the coinherent and reciprocal relations between the Spirit and the Son in opening access for us to the Father and in sealing the efficacy of his atoning propitiation within us. In the fourth Gospel our Lord spoke of the Holy Spirit as the *Paraclete* whom he sends to act in his place. The Spirit is so intimately one with Christ in his being and activity as the incarnate Son of God that he is, as it were, Christ's *Other Self* through whose presence in us Christ himself is present to us. The Spirit seals our adoption in Christ as children of God and unites us to Christ in such a way that we are made by grace to share in his filial relation to the Father. The Holy Spirit is the living and life-giving Spirit of God who actualises the self-giving of God to us in his Son, and resonates and makes fruitful within us the priestly, atoning and intercessory activity of Christ on our behalf. Thus it is worth noting that when St Paul, in the eighth chapter of his Epistle to the Romans, speaks of the interceding or intervening activity of the Holy Spirit on our behalf, he actually employs strengthened forms of the very terms used to speak of the vicarious activity of Christ. Through the Holy Spirit the heavenly advocacy and intercession of Christ our great High Priest are made to echo inaudibly within us, so that our praying and worshipping of God in the Spirit are upheld and made effective by him through a relation of God to himself.

We recall that the oneness in being and activity between the incarnate Son and God the Father means that we cannot but speak in a significant way of the sacrifice of the Father in and with the sacrifice of the Son, whom he did not spare but freely gave up for our sake. Thus we must speak of the passion or suffering of God himself. It was not of course the Father but the Son who was incarnate and suffered on the cross, but the distinctiveness of the Persons of the Father and of the Son, does not imply any division in the oneness of their being, or in the oneness of their activity, for God's being and act are inseparable. We must think likewise of the oneness in activity as well as the oneness in being between the Holy Spirit and God the Father and God the Son. Although it was not the Spirit but the Son who became incarnate and died for us on the cross, there is no conflict between the being and act of the Spirit and the being and act of Christ, for there is an unbroken relationship of being and act between them even in the fearful passion and dereliction of Christ at Calvary. The coinherent relation between the Spirit and the Son implies that the Holy Spirit was afflicted with the affliction of Christ, and suffered with him like the Father in his atoning sacrifice. We recall again that it was through the eternal Spirit that Christ offered himself in atoning oblation to the Father.

Just as we must think of the incarnation of the Son and his atoning work as the Mediator between God and man as taking place within the life of God, so we must surely think of the vicarious operation of the Spirit in indivisible conjunction with the vicarious activity of Christ as falling within the life of God. This reinforces the truth that it is not only the oneness in being between the incarnate Son and God the Father, but the oneness in being between the Holy Spirit and God the Father that constitutes the all-important ontological bond between the trinitarian relations of God's self-revealing activity toward us in the Gospel and the trinitarian relations immanent in the one eternal being of God. We have also to take into our understanding of this the oneness of their activity with one another and with God the Father in effecting atonement, for the atoning act reaches from the historical life and death of Jesus into the eternal being of God, and thereby bridges the chasm of alienation between man and God.

To repeat, it is through the incarnation and atonement effected by the conjoint activity of Christ and the Holy Spirit that God has opened the door for us to enter into his holy presence and know him as he really is in himself in his triune being. In this two-way movement of atoning propitiation whereby God draws near to us and draws us near to himself, the access to the Father given to us through the grace of the Lord Jesus Christ and in the communion of the Holy Spirit is such that we are enabled, quite astonishingly and beyond any worth or capacity of our own, to participate, creaturely beings though we are, in the eternal communion and inner relations of knowing and loving within God himself, and know him there as one God in three Persons, Father, Son and Holy Spirit.

The One God and the Triune God

How are we to relate this trinitarian understanding of God to the unitary understanding of God that obtains in traditional Judaism? In the Old Testament itself God is made known through divine revelation as the ever-living Lord, the *I am who I am* in his mighty acts of redemption and *I will be who I will be* in the fulfilment of his covenant mercies and messianic promises. Divine revelation to Israel took a primary once for all form in the giving of the Ten Commandments at Mt Sinai through the mediation of Moses the servant of the Lord, and continued throughout the history of Israel to take place through the Word of God, sometimes sent to people through angelic intermediaries but usually through prophets speaking under the command of God's Word and the inspiration of his Spirit. This did not involve a personal revelation of God, for God himself was not the content of his Word; what took place was rather a manifestation of his holy presence and saving power through his Word. Thus made known in his unique covenant relation with Israel, God was proclaimed, in sharp monotheistic contrast to the polytheism of the heathen nations around Israel, as the one and only God, the Creator of heaven and earth and all there is, beside whom there is no other God. This knowledge of the true God was sustained from age to age both through the witness to himself and his redemptive purpose which God provided in the Levitical liturgy of the Mosaic Tabernacle and the Temple. But it was also quickened and sustained from age to age by the divinely inspired Scriptures which arose out of the priestly and prophetic tradition of Israel. In them the still small voice of the ever-living God continued to echo in the soul of Israel from generation to generation and became indelibly imprinted upon the Jewish mind and character.

The knowing of God in the Old Testament revelation, as it came to be understood and interpreted in the Jewish tradition, had no strictly theological content, so that with the sealing up of vision and the end of prophecy, and with the cessation of the Levitical liturgy after the destruction of Jerusalem, God was worshipped in Judaism as the ineffable, unnameable One, and moral precepts and rabbinical interpretation of them took the place of theological content. Although it was not the case with the God of the Old Testament Scriptures, the God of Judaism seems to have become something of a negative border-line concept. The emphasis in Judaism, derived from the Hebrew Scriptures, is that God himself is utterly incomprehensible whom no one can see and live. He is a God of undifferentiated oneness who cannot be grasped in himself, so that what may be known or said of God does not have to do with what he is in himself but only with his attributes as revealed in his interaction with Israel his covenant people and his external relations with the world. He was revealed above all to Moses as 'The Lord, the Lord God merciful and gracious, slow to anger and abounding in steadfast love and faithfulness, keeping steadfast love for thousands, forgiving iniquity and transgression and sin, but who will by no means clear the guilty, visiting the iniquity of the fathers upon the children and the children's children, to the third and fourth generation.' Thus the conceptual content of the doctrine of the One God in Judaism is derived from the *Torah* or the Mosaic Law, and from the teaching of the prophets, augmented through the interpretative framework of tradition preserved and supplemented in Rabbinic Judaism. God is above all the Creator and Ruler of the universe, the one and only Lord God, whose nature is incorporeal, eternal and omnipotent, characterised by kindness, goodness, justice, holiness and perfection.

For traditional Rabbinic Judaism the idea that the Lord God Almighty is open to human knowing in the inner relations of his transcendent being is just not entertainable. One cannot help but ask whether traditional Judaism at this point has not been influenced by the kind of dualism evident in the writings of Philo Judaeus, the Jewish philosopher of the first century A.D. who put forward an extreme view of God's transcendence in which he claimed that God is quite beyond knowing and even above virtue. At the same time, however, he developed a rather hellenised notion of the *Logos* or Word of God as an intermediary principle between God and the world, which he held to be both the instrument of God's providential control over the creation and the means through which men may know God. From the Christian point of view, what Judaism needs to consider here, in overcoming an extreme form of transcendentalism, is a deeper and more ontological conception of the Word of God.

It is particularly interesting that Martin Buber, the great Jewish philosopher of our own times, should have criticised Protestant modernism, particularly as it has been influenced by Kant, for advancing a negative border-line concept of God, and then filling it out with notions projected from man's existential self-understanding, and so he attacked it for what he called a 'conceptual letting-go of God'. When one asks Buber, however, about his own view of our knowledge of God, he points to the Hebraic tradition of personal meeting with God in which our anthropomorphic notions of God are checked in confrontation with a primary Thou, and stripped of their mythological projections. And when one asks further of Buber how he thinks a conceptual grasp of God can take place, he indicates, with reference to the teaching of Spinoza, that our conceptual grasp of God is of the relations of love immanent in God. That is quite startling, for Buber evidently recognised that if we are really to know God we must somehow grasp him in his internal relations and not just in his external relations. But this is precisely a primary and essential element in the Christian doctrine of the Trinity. Just as we cannot climb up an absolutely smooth rock face without any indentations in it for our fingers and toes to get a hold on it, so we are unable to have any conceptual grasp of God if his being is characterised by sheer undifferentiated oneness. Such a God could only be open to a purely apophatic or negative approach, when any knowing of him would be a form of unknowing, and when it would not be possible for anyone to enter into the kind of personal relations with him demanded by the Primary Thou.

The problem to which Martin Buber pointed in his criticism of modern Protestant theology is one that arises out of the dualist metaphysics of Immanuel Kant in his radical distinction between things in themselves and things as they appear to us, and thus in his thesis that we cannot know things in their internal, but only in their external, relations. That is why Kant held that what we call the laws of nature are not derived from the inherent rational structures of nature but are imposed by us externally upon nature. However, that conception of knowledge has been comprehensively demolished by one of the greatest Jewish thinkers of our times, Albert Einstein, not least in the profound revolution in knowledge brought about by the theory of general relativity. In it he cut behind and destroyed the dualist ways of thinking within which Kant and the Enlightenment operated, for in no authentic scientific inquiry can empirical data be interpreted in terms of a preconceived and independent system of ideas. He showed that at every level of nature and of human knowledge rational and empirical elements are inseparably integrated, so that authentic knowing in any field of inquiry is established only through penetrating into its internal relations and bringing them to adequate expression.

We are not concerned here with the implications of all this for scientific knowledge of the world of space and time, but it is worth noting that this Einsteinian correction of the theory of knowledge cannot but have the effect of undermining the dualist patterns of thought that led to the isolation of the doctrine of the triune God from the doctrine of the one God. In fact it reinforces the unitary way of thinking which was established in Christian theology through the formulation of the Nicene *homoousion* which overthrew the dualist ways of thinking dominant in the Hellenistic culture of the ancient world, and made room for the formulation of the Christian doctrine of the Holy Trinity. It is to be hoped that Einstein's contribution to the nature of all rational and scientific knowledge may help Jewish and Christian approaches to the doctrine of God at least to draw closer to one another, if only in their rejection of any dualist split between God as he is in himself and God as he appears to be in his revelation. As I see it, this will involve on the part of Jews as well as on the part of Christians a deeper appreciation of the fact that God himself is the content of his revelation, and that the Word of God is not just a Word about God but God addressing us in person and communicating himself to us. A rapprochement of this kind seems in fact to be happening today in the many congregations of Messianic Jews that have appeared, which, in addition to the growing cooperation between Jewish and Christian biblical scholarship, is bound to have a remedial effect in Christian understanding of the Bible. Crucial to this rapprochement will be the illuminating effect of reconciliation as the inner dynamic of God's self-revelation, for there is no way of really knowing God without being reconciled to him.

Necessity of the Trinity for Understanding the Atonement

Hitherto we have been thinking mainly of the necessity of the atonement for our knowledge of God as Holy Trinity, for it is only through the Son and in the Spirit that *we have access to the Father*, and thus to knowledge of him as Father, Son and Holy Spirit in himself. Now, however, we must also think of the Holy Trinity as necessary for our understanding of the atonement, for through the Son and in the Spirit *God has given himself to us* as Father, Son and Holy Spirit. Our thought has pivoted upon the all-important ontological connection between the economic Trinity and the immanent Trinity expressed by the *homoousion* which applies not only to the relations of the Son and the Spirit to the Father but to inner relations of the Trinity as a whole. This formulates the belief that what God is toward us in his revealing and saving acts as Father, Son and Holy Spirit, he is antecedently and eternally in himself, but also that what God is antecedently and eternally in himself as Father, Son and Holy Spirit he is toward us in his revealing and saving acts in Christ and in the Holy Spirit. The point that needs emphasis now is that since God has communicated himself to us in this three-fold way as Father, Son and Holy Spirit, the Trinity belongs to the inner heart of the Christian message of salvation: perfect communion with God means perfect salvation. In other words, unless our salvation derives from the one ultimate being of God who is Father, Son and Holy Spirit eternally in himself, it is finally empty of divine validity and saving power.

So far as belief in the Lord Jesus Christ as Saviour is concerned it is clear that unless there is an unbroken continuity of divine presence and activity between Christ and God, then in the last analysis, Jesus Christ, with all he stands for, is irrelevant for the ultimate destiny of men and women. Unless Jesus Christ is God himself, God the Son incarnate, then the God proclaimed to us in the Gospel is not a God who loves us to the uttermost, but a God whose love falls short of identifying himself with us in Jesus Christ to the extent of actually becoming one with us in and through him. Only God can forgive sins, so that unless Christ is God, his word of forgiveness is empty of any divine substance. Unless Christ is of one and the same being as God, as well as of one and the same being as ourselves, then the atoning sacrifice of Christ on the cross for us and our salvation is in fact without divine validity or saving power.

The New Testament makes it quite clear that the Lord Jesus Christ is the Saviour of the world only if he is God. The acts of Jesus Christ throughout the whole of his life on earth, and in his death and resurrection are saving acts only if they are divine acts. Once again, that was the evangelical significance of the *homoousion* formulated at the Council of Nicaea. Unless there is a relation of oneness in being and act between Jesus Christ and the eternal God, then the bottom falls out of the Gospel message of salvation, and we are still in the grip of our sins. With the deity of Christ, the very essence of the Gospel was at stake. Thus the *homoousion* gave final expres-

sion to the fact that in the Lord Jesus Christ God has wholly
and unconditionally committed himself to us in the incarnation of his Son, so that all he eternally is and will be as God
Almighty is irrevocably pledged in the birth, life, death and
resurrection of Jesus Christ for us and our salvation.

So far as our belief in the Holy Spirit is concerned, it is also
clear that unless there is an unbroken continuity of presence
and activity between the Holy Spirit and God, then in the last
analysis the Holy Spirit and all his manifold operations can
have no saving significance for us. Unless the Holy Spirit is
himself God, then he does not actually give us communion
with God or mediate to us his redeeming and sanctifying
presence in and through himself. Hence the *homoousion* has
also been applied rightly to the Holy Spirit, in expressing the
truth that there is an unbroken relation in being and act
between him and God, as well as between Christ and God,
and an unbroken relation in being and act between the Spirit
and Christ. He is perfectly one with God the Father, and with
God the Son, in being and act, and in him God confronts us
human beings with nothing less than himself. The Holy
Spirit is not just some divine force emanating from God but
different from him, not some sort of action at a distance or
some kind of gift detachable from God, for God *is* Spirit. In
fact, the Holy Spirit is the transcendent freedom of God to be
present to us in such a way as to realise our relationship with
God as the creative and sustaining Source of our being and
life. He is the sanctifying, life-giving and redeeming outreach
of God toward us, drawing us into communion with himself,
undergirding that in the form of a relation of God to himself,
for he is not only God coming to us but God dwelling in us
and upholding us from below in a saving communion with
himself. In him God gives us nothing less than himself: in
him the divine Gift and the divine Giver are identical.

It clearly belongs to the very essence of the Gospel of
salvation that through the Lord Jesus Christ and the Holy
Spirit God has communicated himself to us in atoning propitiation and saving power. This is a threefold self-communication of God to us in unreserved love, in which the Father,
the Son and the Holy Spirit, while other than one another in

the distinctiveness of their Persons and Acts, are perfectly and indivisibly one, for no divine Person is what he is apart from the others. The Father is not properly Father apart from the Son and the Spirit, and the Son is not properly Son apart the Father and the Spirit, and the Spirit is not properly Spirit apart from the Father and the Son. They are completely at one in their mutual indwelling, containing and interpenetrating of one another. This triune relation between the Father, the Son and the Holy Spirit applies to all their activity, not least in the movement of atoning propitiation and expiation whereby all who come to the Father through the Son and in the Holy Spirit are redeemed and saved from sin and death and judgment. Thus belief in the Holy Trinity does not have to do simply with our knowledge of God as he is in his inner life and being, but with the very substance of the Gospel of salvation grounded in and flowing from the very love which God eternally is in himself. It is indeed God's threefold giving of himself to us as Father, Son and Holy Spirit that is our salvation. This is succinctly and beautifully expressed in the benediction: 'The grace of the Lord Jesus Christ, and the love of God, and the communion of the Holy Spirit, be with you all.' As such, devotion to one God as Father, Son and Holy Spirit belongs to the inner structure of our Christian faith and worship, while the doctrine of the Unity and Trinity of God constitutes the fundamental grammar of Christian theology.

CPSIA information can be obtained
at www.ICGtesting.com
Printed in the USA
BVOW00s1152271016
466053BV00009B/153/P